THE WONDER OF
THE EUCHARIST

The Wonder of the Eucharist

Fr Ken Barker MGL

Modotti Press

Modotti Press, An imprint of Connor Court Publishing Pty Ltd

Copyright © Fr Ken Barker MGL 2015

ALL RIGHTS RESERVED. This book contains material protected under International and Federal Copyright Laws and Treaties. Any unauthorised reprint or use of this material is prohibited. No part of this book may be reproduced or transmitted in any form or by any means, electronic or mechanical, including photocopying, recording, or by any information storage and retrieval system without express written permission from the publisher.

PO Box 224W
Ballarat VIC 3350
sales@connorcourt.com
www.connorcourt.com

Nihil Obstat
Rev Warrick Tonkin BA, DipEd, BTh, BTheol, M.Ed
Censor Deputatis
Imprimatur
Most Rev Christopher Prowse DD STD
Archbishop of Canberra and Goulburn

ISBN: 9781925138580

Cover painting by Fr David Tremble MGL
and cover design by Br Lawrence Yuen MGL

Printed in Australia

CONTENTS

Foreword	viii
Introduction	x

PART I WORD AND WORSHIP

1:	Encounter with Christ	3
2:	The Power of the Word	10
3:	Worship	18

PART II SACRIFICE

4:	The Last Supper	29
5:	Christ: Broken and Given	34
6:	Self-giving Love for us	43
7:	Drinking the Cup	50

PART III COMMUNION

8:	Intimacy with Jesus	58
9:	Sanctification	63
10:	The Blood of Jesus Washes us Clean	69
11:	Communion in the Body of Christ	74
12:	The Washing of the Feet	82

PART IV PRESENCE

13:	The Real Presence	89
14:	Eucharistic Adoration	101

PART V MISSION

15: Proclaiming the Good News	113
16: Healing Power	119
17: Sharing in the Victory of Jesus	126
18: Intercession	134
19: Bread for the Hungry	139
20: Reconciliation and Peace	148
Endnotes	157

Acknowledgements

I wish to thank Selina Hasham for reading over the whole text and making suggestions. I am also grateful to Fr David Tremble MGL for permission to use his painting on the front page, and also for Lawrence Yuen MGL for designing the page. Most of all I have a debt of gratitude to all those many people over the years who through their profound faith in the Eucharist have inspired me to have a deep love for this mystery.

FOREWORD

Fr Ken Barker is a gifted and well known Catholic priest in Australia. I find him a great example of a priest truly blessed by the Holy Spirit. His gifts in Catholic evangelisation have seen him travel throughout Australia and the world proclaiming the Good News of Jesus Christ with great spiritual power.

Among Fr Barker's many gifts is writing. In *The Wonder of the Eucharist* he explores in a popular and pastoral manner the great Sacrament of the Eucharist. It is as if we are listening to his deep and personal reflections on the Eucharist. He describes the Eucharist as the "beautiful diamond" of the Church. It is refreshing to read of his "Eucharistic amazement", as St John Paul II would describe it.

It is out of profound love of the Eucharist that Fr Barker writes about the Eucharist. He reflects: "Having celebrated the Eucharist with warm devotion for forty years as a priest, my heart is captivated by this mystery, and held by bonds of love."

The text is instructive but not technical in a dense theological way. The book has a drawing power of its own. It would help those who find going to Mass somewhat routine and would like it to be otherwise. This is one of Fr Barker's purposes in writing the book. He aims for the reader to encounter afresh the "awesome mystery" of the Eucharist.

I was particularly pleased to read of Fr Barker's reflections on Eucharistic adoration and devotion. I have noticed in this area increased Catholic focus worldwide, and particularly here in Australia. Perhaps surprisingly, this is evident especially amongst the youth. The World Youth Days I have attended seem to illustrate this. Young people have indicated to me one highlight of the World Youth Day is the Eucharistic adoration led by the Pope. To be in prolonged and prayerful silence with over a million people from all over the world in the evening Eucharistic adoration led by the Pope is an unforgettable experience.

Also, today's increase in Eucharistic adoration chapels attached to our parishes throughout Australia and elsewhere is also fascinating to observe. In our busy world, times of silent Eucharistic adoration are so very helpful to the growth of people's prayer lives and help depth their everyday activities.

As is his style, Fr Barker has peppered his book with personal stories and anecdotes from his pastoral experience and reading. I was delighted to see his reference, for example, to the former Archbishop of Saigon, Cardinal Francis Xavier Nguyen Van Thuan. He spent many years in prison in Vietnam because of his strong Catholic faith. It was his profound love and wonder of the Eucharist that matured him in desperate times. The fact that his parents lived in Australia in their latter years and his sister still lives in Canberra, helps us appreciate his saintly good example at a more personal level.

My prayer is that this wonderful new book by Fr Barker on the Eucharist will be read widely. Let us be amazed with Fr Barker on the gift of the Eucharist. May we more deeply encounter Jesus as we read his reflective meditations on the wonder of the Eucharist. By so doing we will enter the inner chambers of the Church's spiritual treasury. After all, as quoted by Fr Barker from the documents of Vatican II, "in the most blessed Eucharist is contained the whole spiritual good of the Church." (*Presbyterorum ordinis*, 5)

Archbishop Christopher Prowse
Catholic Archbishop of Canberra and Goulburn

INTRODUCTION

Many Catholics who are faithful in attending Mass have not yet discovered the wonder of the Eucharist. Mass can be a routine affair, a formal ritual, with which we are very familiar. But apart from a few devotional prayers many are not sure how best to participate. They are not really in touch with the nature of the Eucharist as a sacrifice and what it means to offer themselves in the Mass. A high proportion of Mass-goers believe in the real presence as a special miracle that takes place, and are grateful for the spiritual food of communion. But they may not have given much thought to the real significance of this celebration for our individual or communal lives. This book is a humble attempt to help those Catholics who are looking for a way to deepen in their appreciation of this awesome mystery. Our regular celebration of the Mass is a wonderful privilege, but all too often it is simply something we do because we implicitly know it is good for us, but without much depth of reflection about its significance. If this book aids just one person to deepen in his or her participation in the Eucharist it will have achieved its goal.

Writing is not always a totally altruistic exercise. In this instance I am well aware that I am writing for myself as well as for others. Having celebrated the Eucharist with warm devotion for forty years as a priest, my heart is captivated by this mystery, and held by bonds of love. I have allowed myself to be possessed by the mystery. When I celebrate the Mass and also when I adore Jesus in the exposed Blessed Sacrament, I am drawn back again and again into the embrace of our Saviour. However, I feel very inadequate to be able to articulate the meaning of what is in fact the love of my life. I have felt prompted to write as a way of clarifying in my own mind why I have been so caught up in this immense gift of Love. Of course, a mystery like the

Eucharist is not meant to be analysed and unravelled. It is far more important to simply be captured by its supernatural enchantment. Yet there is part of every human being that wants to know "why this is so?" Faith seeks understanding, not so that we can master the mystery; God forbid I would even think that was possible; but so that I may more consciously and actively participate more fully in its wonder and inherent beauty.

I, like many Catholics, need to periodically shake myself and open my eyes again to the wonder of the Eucharist. Was Vatican II exaggerating when it said, "The most holy Eucharist contains the Church's entire spiritual wealth?"[1] What an enormous claim! Christ himself, the living bread, through his own flesh, "offers life to all". He is the Bread of Life. Was the Catholic Catechism in earnest when it said, "the Eucharist is the sum and summary of our faith"?[2] We cannot ignore such an all-embracing proclamation. My aim is not to cover comprehensively every aspect of this mystery. How could that be possible? I simply want to do what I can to open up this treasure of our faith, and help us rediscover it in a fresh way.

As I was thinking about the immense riches we have in the Eucharist, and was preparing to write, I found a reluctance in me. Who could do justice to such a wonderful mystery? All the ink that has been spilt and the millions of words typed, as faith-filled people have laboured to open up the meaning of this incredible treasure. What more could be said? That reflection helped me to realize that I would not be able to say anything really new, but at the same time it could be useful to share humbly some of the insights about the Eucharist that have impacted me over the years.

On this latter point I want to express my indebtedness to Fr Raniero Cantalamessa for his reflections on the Eucharist which he has offered as preacher to the Papal Household. I am referring particularly to his preaching on the Eucharist which was compiled into a book entitled *The Eucharist: Our Sanctification*. And I am also grateful for his Advent sermons in 2004 and his Lenten Sermons in 2005, in which he reflected upon the ancient hymns, *Adoro te Devote* and *Ave Verum*. These teachings have influenced sections of this book, and I acknowledge this with gratitude.

Approaching the Eucharistic mystery could be likened to gazing upon a beautiful diamond. The precious diamond is highly valuable and exquisite in beauty. Its beauty yields itself to us over time, as we gaze upon it. A finely cut diamond shows up its brilliance as the light of the sun shines upon it bringing out an inner beauty. As you turn the diamond around and look upon it from a different perspective another facet of its inner mystery is revealed. And then from another perspective the light brings out a further brilliant aspect. That is the way I intend to approach the mystery in this book. The reader will notice that I have in fact managed to put some order into the chapters, but initially I simply allowed myself to be captivated by one facet of the diamond and explore that. Then I turned the diamond a little and held it up to the light and found another dimension as yet hidden. This is partly why the book is called "the wonder" of the Eucharist. It is an attempt to capture something of what Pope John Paul II encouraged in the Year of the Eucharist – a "Eucharistic amazement!"

Given this way of proceeding it means that the reader can dip into the book at any stage and hopefully find something to ponder. However, by the grace of God I have been able to divide the work into five parts, which are each essential for an appreciation of Eucharist. Firstly, there is an introductory section on the place of the word of God and the importance of worship. Then the next three parts cover the main concepts of the Eucharist that occupy theologians: sacrifice, communion, and presence. The final part situates the Eucharist in the mission of the Church in the world today. In each of these parts I have gathered together those perspectives gained from looking upon the diamond which seem to fit most under that heading.

I am aware of the cultural context in which we find ourselves and the vast number of Catholics who have never come anywhere near the Mass for years. I am hoping that this book may help some who are on a serious search to have another look and be amazed at what they find. This is an age when it seems everyone is looking for the secret formula for a life worth living. Maybe never before in the history of the human race have so many been aspiring for a richer way of life, and spending endless amounts of time, money and talent in seeking to find the elusive answer to what will fulfil the deepest longing of the human heart. There is a quest for "more than this"; but most are quietly frustrated, unable to find the gold they sense is yet to be gained. They struggle through life without a clear understanding of why they are here, and without any real future direction.

Maybe there has never been a climate more conducive to the proclamation of Jesus as the fullness of life. He said, "I have come that you may have life, and have it to the full" (Jn 10:10). That is the quest of almost every person I meet. We want to find a higher plane of living, not by joining the angels, but by becoming fully what we can be as human beings. We want our human lives to count for something. We want to make a difference. And when we have gone, we want to have left a legacy, by which we can be remembered. But what is this fullness of life that Jesus offers? How is it to be found? More things? Experiencing more excitement? Enjoying more entertainment? Travelling the world? If these are our absolutes, ultimately we are left empty, unfulfilled.

Many don't realise that the only way a human being can be fulfilled is through self-giving love, and the source of all love is God. We don't realise that we are hungering for God. He is the answer to the deepest longing of our hearts. Yet most seem to be setting up their life quest without him. The narcissistic voice within us does not want to know the real secret for human living; that we find love in the cross of Jesus. If we are to discover what it is to love, then we need to die on the cross with him. Ouch! That is not a popular message today.

We want to have fullness of life, but without the dying that is necessary to attain it. Jesus showed the way to fullness of life when he died on the cross for us. This is the heart of the message, but not many want to hear it. God is love! But love hurts. The proclamation of the cross has never been popular. Paul complained that "the Jews demand miracles and the Greeks look for wisdom, and here we are proclaiming a crucified Christ; to the Jews a stumbling block and to the pagans madness. But to those who are called, it is the power and wisdom of God" (1 Cor 1:22-23). This is the perennial message. "The language of the cross may be illogical to those who are not on the way to salvation, but those of us who are ... see it as God's power to save" (1 Cor1:18).

This is the essence of the mystery of the Eucharist. We have revealed to us the saving love of Jesus who died on the cross for us, and we are drawn into this mystery of love so that we go through an interior revolution. We change from being self-centred to being other centred. Our lives are no longer about "getting", but about "giving". And that is when we come fully alive as human beings.

PART I

WORD AND WORSHIP

The two parts which in a sense go to make up the Mass, viz. The liturgy of the Word and the Eucharistic liturgy, are so closely connected with each other that they form but one single act of worship. (SC 56)

When your words came, I devoured them: your word was my delight and the joy of my heart. (Jer 15:16)

1

ENCOUNTER WITH CHRIST

"Was it not ordained that the Son of Man should suffer before entering into his glory?" (Lk 24:26)

On the Road to Emmaus

The Eucharist is an encounter with the risen Christ bringing hope to all disciples "on the way", no matter what shape we are in, and how far we have moved from our original fervour. We meet Jesus in the word proclaimed, and in the breaking of the bread. Our eyes are opened again, and with new hope, we want to share this good news with others. The Emmaus story told by Luke illustrates this aspect of the Eucharistic mystery beautifully.

Two of the disciples were walking away from Jerusalem towards Emmaus, a village seven miles away. We are told it was the same day the tomb was found empty, the first day of the week. It is significant that they had turned their backs on Jerusalem, and were "walking away". This movement is in contrast to the whole structure of Luke's gospel, in which the journey of Jesus and his disciples is deliberately *towards* Jerusalem where salvation would be attained. Then in the Acts of the Apostles, which was Luke's sequel to the gospel, the disciples, empowered by the Spirit go forth from Jerusalem to proclaim the gospel to the ends of the earth. But these two disciples were leaving Jerusalem not with the joy of the good news but to escape from the shame and humiliation of the experience of the cross. They were obviously disillusioned and without hope because of what they had witnessed as they watched Jesus die on Calvary. For them it was the end of the messianic dream. As they bemoaned the tragedy of the death of Jesus, they were reinforcing their sadness and self-pity. Significantly, Jesus drew alongside them, and they did not recognise him. How easily the experience of loss, disappointment, and tragedy in our lives can leave us so dispirited we do not recognise the presence of Christ with us. Our eyes are not open to him, and we huddle together in a self-enclosed "pity party", rather than be aware of his closeness and consolation.

When Jesus asked them what they were talking about, we are told "they stopped short, their faces downcast". Stripped of joy and hope, Cleopas says, "You must be the only person staying in Jerusalem who does not know the things that have been happening there these last few days". The reader can't help but see the irony as Jesus asks, "What things?" And then Cleopas elaborates on all they had hoped about Jesus of Nazareth. Note that Cleopas has all the facts he needs to be fully alive with the good news. He tells the story: Jesus of Nazareth proved he was a great prophet by what he said and did; then the chief priests and leaders handed him over to be sentenced to death, and had him crucified. It was now the third day and some women from their group went to the tomb in the early morning and came back with the story that the tomb was empty and angels had told them that he was alive. Some of their friends had been to the tomb and verified what the women had said. But they saw nothing of Jesus. Amazingly Cleopas and his friend knew the content of the *kerygma*, the basic proclamation of the good news of God's saving love in Jesus. But it had not impacted their lives. They had given into despair and were now leaving town fearful that they may suffer the same fate as Jesus.

Maybe these two disciples represent for us those in today's church who have heard the catechetical truths but are still disconnected from the living person of the risen Jesus. Their journey in the church is a sort of "grey pragmatism", and in the face of trouble and difficulties they struggle forward with a dogged stoicism, weighed down by a feeling of defeat and a sense that we are in a losing game. Their journey is moving them away from Jerusalem; seeking to escape from the unbearable pain of feeling there is no meaning in it all anymore. Jesus is walking with them. He is in our midst always. But they do not recognise him.

Or maybe they represent for us those who have experienced the shadow of the cross fall upon their lives through unexpected calamity or bewildering loss. In their shattered hearts they are struggling to make sense of it all. Not realising what they are doing, they turn their back on their real source of consolation. Even when Jesus is in their presence they cannot recognise him. They prevail upon others to comfort them, but fail to see the one who is the greatest comfort of all.

The Word of life

Jesus gently rebukes these disciples, "Was it not ordained that Christ should suffer and so enter into his glory?" The implication is that just as it was for the Master, so it will be for the disciples. He opens up for them the word of God given through the scriptures which were about himself. He explains how the whole of scripture was pointing towards his suffering and death on the cross, and that rather than being a disaster it was the fulfilment of all that had been promised. Jesus interpreted the prophecies of the Old Testament to show them that it was all about him, the Christ. It is there that all the promises of God are given and prefigured, whether explicitly or implicitly, for their fulfilment in Christ. It all leads towards the crucified and risen Christ. Later the two disciples remembered how their "hearts burned within them" as Jesus explained the scriptures to them.

Most commentators say that this whole Emmaus journey is deliberately presented by Luke in a Eucharistic key. The disciples are down-hearted on their journey. They had given up the search for meaning in what had happened, and were walking away from the gift of God's mercy and goodness. That there are two together reminds us of the promise of Jesus, "Where two or three are gathered in my name I am in the midst of them" (Mt 18:20). Eucharist is profoundly communal. Together we are on a journey where we constantly need an injection of hope. The liturgy of the word is a major way this happens. As on the road to Emmaus Christ himself speaks to us on our way, expounds to us all that is about him in the scriptures and opens our hearts to a deeper level of conversion, so we can encounter him more intimately in the "breaking of the bread".

Their Eyes were Opened

When the three travellers drew near the village of Emmaus, Jesus, who they still did not recognise, made as if to go on. It was not just that he "appeared to be going further", as translated in the RSV. The Greek is more suggestive. It means he "*pretended* to be going further". He had unfolded for them the plan of God in the scriptures. Now they had to respond. They did so generously, "Stay with us for it is towards evening, and the day is far spent." This invitation indicates that through hearing the word of God their faith had been stirred in a new way. With the shadows of the passing day growing longer and the darkness of their clouded spirit still hanging over them, they had experienced "a ray of light which rekindled their hope and led their hearts to yearn for the fullness of light".[3] Those words "Stay with us, Lord" are still the cry of all hearts yearning for encounter with the risen Jesus in Eucharist today.

The story leads quickly to a climax. Jesus sits at table with them, and "he took the bread, said the blessing; then he broke it and handed it to them". At this moment "their eyes were opened and they recognised him". He had vanished, but it did not matter. They had seen him and continued to know him. They returned quickly to Jerusalem, a complete reversal of their previous direction. They reclaimed their status as genuine disciples, no longer full of fear and dismay, no longer disillusioned and in disarray. All was changed. They rushed to tell the other disciples what had happened on the road, and "how they had recognised him at the breaking of the bread". Eucharist is a profound encounter with the risen Christ. These disciples had seen the face of Jesus, as the one who had been travelling with them. But even though he immediately disappeared, he would "stay" with them in the "breaking of the bread", through which their eyes had been opened.

The Eucharistic Encounter

In a similar way the risen Jesus is walking with us. Through daily reading of the scriptures, and especially in the liturgy of the word Christ speaks to us on the way, and our faith is stirred up, as we are made ready for the Eucharistic encounter. But the first encounter is in the word. We need to have a deep hunger for the word of God. May our hearts burn within us as the Holy Spirit convicts us of the truth of his word. When the priest, in the person of Christ, takes the bread and wine, says the blessing prayer, and breaks the bread, and gives it to us for our food, our eyes are opened. The liturgy of the Eucharist is built around this fundamental fourfold action, done by the priest, in imitation of Jesus, with all the faithful participating – taking the bread and wine (offertory), praying the blessing prayer (Eucharistic prayer), breaking the bread (*fractio*) and giving the body and blood (communion). In the early Church the whole action was simply called "the breaking of the bread". Unfortunately in contemporary liturgy the actual rite of the breaking of the bread can sometimes be hidden and its meaning obscured. If possible it is good to make the symbol speak loudly to help remind participants of the depth of its meaning.

We encounter the risen Christ, who by his word and the food of his very self, brings hope to our hearts. The many crosses of life will bring disappointment, when we are let down by others, or fail ourselves, or face bewildering suffering. The Evil One plays in this field. He fosters disillusionment and discouragement, prompting us to give up, and "throw in the towel". If we allow that disposition to take hold, we enter into darkness, and may find ourselves in the pit of despondency, a prevailing sadness and loss of zest for life. Too long in that state leads to despair. All the while the risen Christ is present. The Mass is great therapy when this debilitating dynamic is at work within us. Like the despondent disciples on the road to Emmaus Jesus will speak to us and lift us out of our self-made heaviness, and put hope into our hearts once again.

Encounter with Suffering

Before opening the scriptures which set their hearts on fire, Jesus asked a probing question, "Was it not ordained that the Son of Man should suffer before entering his glory?" From our perspective we know that the cross was all part of God's saving plan. But who can be blithely light-hearted about the sober implications of this reality? Like the two disciples we will necessarily experience suffering on our journey. But the presence of Jesus with us in our situation is a guarantee of hope, of an eventual end to darkness, and that, in spite of present appearances, all will finally be well. The core of our faith is the man, Jesus, hanging on the cross in pain, shame and confusion, his life collapsed into failure, crying out in anguish, "My God, my God, why have you abandoned me." At that moment, most of all, he was in solidarity with every human being who suffers, with those who have lost all sense of purpose and meaning in life. But, we know that despair, anguish, emptiness and darkness are not the end of the story. He rose from the dead and he is now with us, to give assurance when we too collapse into darkness.

The self-offering love of Jesus on the cross overcame death. It brought new hope when it seemed there was no hope. But the cross does not protect us from pain or provide an escape from it. Rather the grace is there to face the pain, and to go through it with love. When disaster strikes, and it surely will, rather than allow ourselves to be dragged down in a vortex of self-pity, and become bitter and resentful, we can lift our hearts to God and make our "yes" to him. Jesus in the Garden of Gethsemane was faced with this decision. Rather than succumb to the temptation to despair he freely embraced the coming ordeal to the bitter end, so we could be redeemed. We are all faced with our Gethsemane experience at one time or another. We can opt to run away, escaping into alcohol, drugs, or sexual licence, losing ourselves in fantasy, or we can look the reality in the face, and endure it with hope. The dawning of the resurrection may not yet be apparent, but its coming is real all the same. Eucharist makes present this paschal mystery, and helps us to live it. As the psalmist says, "With the night there are tears; but joy comes with the dawn." (Ps 30:6)

2

THE POWER OF THE WORD

"All scripture is inspired by God and is useful for teaching, for reproof, for correction, and for training in righteousness." (2 Tim 3:16)

The Two Tables of the Bread of Life

The Emmaus story alerts us to the context of the Mass as a journey together as disciples during which we encounter Jesus. There are two major moments in this encounter – the liturgy of the word and the liturgy of the Eucharist. These two parts of the overall liturgy of the Mass are both essential for its integrity. The document on liturgy at Vatican Council II declared that "the liturgy of the word and the Eucharistic liturgy are so closely connected that they form one single act of worship"[4]. This was an enormous change in Catholic thinking. Prior to that time the readings from scripture and the sermon were seen simply as a prelude and preparation for the main drama. In those days the word and sacrament were seen as very distinct and easily separated. But with the twentieth century biblical renewal, the sacred scriptures were again brought into the centre of Catholic worship, and the proclamation of the word was given greater prominence. We claimed again that we are a people of the word of God. Another document of the Council had this to say: "The Church has always venerated the divine scriptures as she venerated the body of the

Lord, in so far as she never ceases, particularly in the sacred liturgy, to partake of the bread of life and to offer it to the faithful from the one table of the word of God and the body of Christ."[5] This is exciting language and we are still absorbing the significance of it.

There are two "tables" at the Mass from which we are nourished and strengthened by Jesus, who is the bread of life: the table of the word and the table of the Eucharist. This is why architects of contemporary sanctuaries seek to place the ambo, with the lectern, from which the word is proclaimed, in a prominent place, somewhat juxtaposed with the altar from which we receive the body of Christ. While the altar of sacrifice is rightfully central, we receive the same bread of life, Christ himself, from both tables. The word of God is our food for living. As a people we gather for this nourishment which "enlightens the mind, strengthens the will and fires the hearts of men and women with the love of God". We are told that "such is the force and power of the word of God" that it brings "support and vigour", as well as "strength for faith, food for the soul and a pure and lasting fount of spiritual life".[6]

The Unity of Word and Eucharist

This unity of the word and Eucharist is emphasised also in the classic text from chapter 6 in John's gospel. Later we will look at this text as a strong witness to Jesus as the bread of life, really present under the appearance of bread after the consecration. But in the first part of that chapter the author is drawing a comparison between Jesus and Moses, between the one who spoke face to face with God (*cf.* Ex 33:11) and the one who is nearest to the Father's heart and now makes God known (*cf.* Jn 1:18). Jesus' discourse speaks of the gift of the bread of life, the manna from heaven, which Moses obtained for his people. This represented the Torah, the word of God given in the old covenant. Jesus was claiming to be the new bread of life himself.

He is *the* Word made flesh come into the world to bring fullness of life. He says, "It was not Moses who gave you bread from heaven. It is my Father who gives you the bread from heaven, the true bread; for the bread of God is that which comes down from heaven and gives life to the world" (Jn 6:32). He is substituting the word of old, given in the law, with himself, the Word of life. All who believe in him will live; "the law has become a person. When we encounter Jesus we feed on the living God himself, so to speak, we truly eat the 'bread from heaven'."[7]

There is one unbreakable bond between the word and Eucharist. Pope Benedict explains:

> The Word and Eucharist are so deeply bound together that we cannot understand one without the other: the word of God sacramentally takes flesh in the event of the Eucharist. The Eucharist opens us to understanding of scripture, just as scripture for its part illumines and explains the mystery of the Eucharist.[8]

The "*Dabar*" of God.

The liturgy of the word is celebrated in the form a dialogue between God and his people. All through salvation history God has been speaking to his people by words and deeds, forming a covenant with them, and calling for their response. This is the dynamic of the liturgy. The readings are not just information about God and his dealings with his people. They are in fact Christ speaking to us, feeding us with his word. The liturgy of the word is a happening event. God is communicating himself to us, offering himself to us as the bread of life, inviting us to dwell in his presence.

In the Church today we need a renewed appreciation of the divine power of the word of God in the readings from scripture and the homily. We need to stand under God's word with awe and reverence, and expect it to bring change to our lives. The Hebrew "*dabar*" means the word in action. The proclaimed word is powerful and dynamic, bringing about the effects it signifies. When the word was spoken by the prophets it was not just to be heard, but to be acted upon. And it contained the inherent power to bring about change in hearts:

> Yes, as the rain and the snow come down from the heavens and do not return without watering the earth, making it yield and giving growth to provide seed for the sower and bread for the eating, so the word that goes from my mouth does not return to me empty, without carrying out my will and succeeding in what it was sent to do. (Is. 55:10-11)

In the gospels when Jesus spoke there was power in his words. Demons fled, people were healed, and many came to repentance, a genuine change of heart. We are told by Mark, "his teaching made a deep impression on them because, unlike the scribes, he taught them with authority" (Mk. 1:22). While Jesus was teaching in the synagogue at Capernaum an evil spirit began to manifest. Jesus delivered the man on the spot. The people were astonished and began to ask themselves what it all meant: "Here is a teaching that is new and with authority behind it: he gives orders even to unclean spirits and they obey him." (Mk. 1:27)

"The word of God is alive and active. It cuts more finely than any double-edged sword" (Heb 12:12-14). If we are open and attentive, the Holy Spirit will convict us of the truth of the word proclaimed and we will be called to a deeper level of repentance and personal transformation. Hearing and responding to the word of God prepares us for full participation in the Eucharistic liturgy. Paul says, "Faith comes from what is preached and what is preached comes from the word of Christ" (Rom 10:17). Like the disciples on the road to Emmaus, if our faith is stirred up from listening to the word of Christ, and our hearts are burning within us, then we will be more open to recognise Christ in the breaking of the bread.

Aim for Conversion

We know that every Eucharist contains all the fruits of the sacrifice of Jesus and these are guaranteed to be made available to us for our sanctification. Then why are we not yet living saints, and why are our communities not yet fully credible witnesses of the love of God revealed in Jesus? The answer is in the lack of faith and conversion in the participants. To go on celebrating the sacraments without allowing the word of God to convert us is simply ritualism and formalism. We believe in the "*ex opere operato*" effect of the sacrament; that the graces of the sacrament are guaranteed to be present. But we sometimes forget the need for the "*ex opera operantis*", that is our own disposition of openness, receptivity, desire, and fire for God and for his will in our lives. By standing under his word and allowing him to convert us more deeply, we are more adequately disposed in our hearts to share in the sacrificial offering and receive the body and blood of the Lord in Holy Communion.

Pope Benedict taught that the privileged place for the word of God is in the liturgy of the Mass itself or in some way related to that celebration. He says, "Just as the adoration of the Eucharist prepares for, accompanies and follows the liturgy of the Eucharist, so too prayerful reading of scripture, personal and communal, prepares for, accompanies and deepens what the Church celebrates when she proclaims the word within a liturgical setting".[9] This is a call to meditate on the readings of the lectionary before, during, and after Mass, allowing the word to shape our hearts and form our minds to be more like that of Christ. I highly recommend the practice of *lectio divina*, prayerfully reading the scriptural word with ever deeper levels of loving attentiveness. We chew over the word, let it sink into our hearts, and allow its power to change us from within. The word of God is meant to recreate our minds, stir our hearts to seek holiness, and give direction to our lives.

Importance of the Homily

In all of this the importance of the homily looms large. In the homily the priest is meant to bring the scriptural message alive in such a way that it "makes the faithful realise that God's word is present and at work in their daily lives".[10] Pope Francis has emphasised strongly the impact of the homily. He says that preaching should "guide the assembly and the preacher to a life-changing communion with Christ in the Eucharist".[11] He sees the homily as "the supreme moment in the dialogue between God and his people which leads up to sacramental communion".[12] Preachers must be on fire with the Spirit, well-prepared with "an attitude of humble and awe-filled veneration of the word".[13] They are to plumb the depth of the scriptural text's meaning and to transmit the intrinsic power of the text being proclaimed. They must live holy lives and be penetrated by the word, so their proclamation in the power of the Spirit will penetrate the hearts of others.

When many of his disciples were leaving Jesus, because of his teaching on the Eucharist, he turned to the Twelve and asked, "Will you also go away?" Peter answered, "To whom shall we go, you have the words of eternal life." Here the Greek for "words" is the plural of *rhema*. It is "the word" for this moment right now, the word that "hits home" immediately, because it speaks prophetically into the existential situation of the listeners. Peter is saying we can't leave you because we would be cut off from your words that give us life. Jesus spoke into the deepest dilemmas of their lives, bringing consolation in affliction, challenge in complacency, healing when wounded and clarity in confusion. This is the task of the homilist. He must know intimately the heart of his listeners, and have compassion for their particular situation, and meet this with a word from the heart of Jesus, the good Shepherd.

The Pope is seeking to restore the gift of *kerygmatic* preaching within the Church. He says preachers may have many flaws and foibles, but "what is essential is that the preacher be certain that God loves him, that Jesus Christ has saved him and that His love is always the last word".[14] This is the heart of the message. Having lived the *kerygma* they must preach it. Paul reminded the Corinthians that when he was with them he did not try to persuade by oratory or by using arguments that come from philosophy. "The only knowledge I claimed to have was about Jesus, and only about him as the crucified Christ." (1 Cor 2:2). Paul was not relying on human wisdom, but the power of God. When we preach Jesus crucified things happen, the Spirit begins to act, faith is awakened, conversion occurs, and God is glorified.

Call to Obedience

The proclamation of the word calls forth a response of "obedience of faith" (Rom 1:5, 16:26). If we really respond to the word with obedient hearts then this will be our sacrifice of praise to God which we offer with the sacrifice of Jesus. If we are allowing the word to really convert us, and together seek to live the word of God, then this is our sacrifice, the gift of ourselves as a community seeking to respond to God's covenant love for us.

We will discuss later how the sacrifice of Jesus was essentially his obedience to the Father's will unto death for our sake. And the Eucharistic action makes this sacrifice of Jesus present. We will also see how the Eucharist is not only about the sacrifice of Jesus; it is also about *our* sacrifice. It is the sacrifice of the whole Church, and of each member of the Church. The word of God calls us to obey. If we really allow ourselves to be impacted by the word we will not just have our ears tickled, nor will we simply feel we have been entertained, or have gained some interesting insights. We will be inspired to obey. We will actually do the will of God. As James exhorts, "Be doers of the word, and not merely hearers who deceive themselves." He goes on to say that if we hear the word and don't act on it we are like a person who looks in a mirror and then wanders away forgetting immediately what they look like. (*cf.* James 1:22-25)

The word obedience is derived from the Latin "ob-audire", which means to listen to, or to hearken to attentively. But in a biblical context this does not mean passive listening, but hearing the word of God and *acting* on it. We honour the Blessed Virgin Mary not only because she heard what the angel said to her, but she obeyed: "Let it be done to me according to your will." Jesus warned us that "It is not those who say 'Lord, Lord' who will enter the kingdom of God, but those who *do the will of my Father in heaven.*" He then used the image of building on sand for those who are not obedient to the word, in contrast to building on rock for those who are obedient. (*cf.* Mt 7:24-27)

All of this means that the liturgy of the word is integral to our offering the Mass. To the extent that we allow the word proclaimed to change our hearts and respond actively to the call of the Lord, to that extent will our Eucharistic celebration be genuine worship, a true sacrifice of praise to God.

3

WORSHIP

"I will sing to the Lord all my life, make music to my God while I live ... I find my joy in the Lord ... Bless the Lord, my soul." (Psalm 104: 33-35)

Worship in Spirit and in Truth

The Eucharist is the Church's highest act of worship. Human beings are designed to worship God. We were created for this. That is how we fulfil our fundamental purpose. If we do not worship, we dysfunction as human beings. St Paul identifies the original sin of humanity as "impiety", the refusal to worship (Rom 1:18). If we refuse to worship God, we will end up worshipping someone or something else; we will fall upon God's creatures and worship them. We will worship money, or power, or pleasure, or an "adorable" person, or sadly even oneself. Worship lifts us out of self-preoccupation, and fascination with the passing things of this world. It centres our hearts entirely on God.

The Mass is a form of *communal* worship. But mere attendance at Mass does not necessarily mean we have actually worshipped God. It may just be a ritual act performed out of habit without the heart being engaged in the act. Jesus complained of his contemporaries, "This people worships with lip service but their hearts are far from me" (Mk 7:6). The woman at the well raised with Jesus the issue of who has the authentic worship; the Samaritans who worshipped on Mt Gerizim or the Jews who worshipped in Jerusalem. Jesus made it clear it is not *where* you worship that matters, nor so much the fine points of the ritual that are used. What is important is that we worship "in spirit and in truth" (Jn 4:22-23). It is not the ritual act of worship itself that makes the worship authentic, but rather the heart of the worshipper. God is not after splendid liturgies with no soul; beautiful rituals which are not expressions of the heart. This is not authentic worship. He first wants *the worshipper*, and then the form and expression of worship can be true. Our ritual actions will only be "in spirit and in truth" when through them we are offering ourselves to him.

A Living Sacrifice of Praise

Our worship in the Eucharistic liturgy will only be as good as our lives are a "living sacrifice of praise" to God. Paul exhorts the Romans, "I appeal to you therefore, brothers and sisters, by the mercies of God to present your bodies as a living sacrifice, holy and acceptable to God, which is your spiritual worship" (Rom 12:1). He goes on to encourage them not be conformed to the thinking of the world, which will lead them to lose this sacrificial attitude, but to allow their minds and hearts to be renewed. Their whole lives are intended to give glory to God. All of their daily living should be a way of worshipping the living God. This is what we mean when we claim that the Eucharist is "the source and summit of the Christian life".[15] Our lives, as Mother Teresa said, are meant to be "something beautiful for God". Paul says, "Whatever you eat, whatever you drink, whatever you do at all, do it for the glory of God" (1 Cor 10:31). The whole moral life is based in this fundamental aspiration that everything we do will give glory to God, and in that sense be an act of worship.

The highest moment of this life of worship which we have as individuals and as a community is Eucharist. We express ritually who we are as a worshipping community and we are deepened in this identity; we are the priestly people who are most ourselves when we are praising God who has called us out of darkness into his wonderful light (*cf.* 1 Pet 2:9). St Augustine eloquently expressed that our praise of God is a way of life:

> 'Sing to the Lord a new song.' Sing with your voice, your mouth, your hearts, sing with befitting behaviour. 'May his praise ring out in the gathering of the saints.' The singer himself is the praise that must be sung. Do you want to praise God? You are the praise that must be said. You are his praise if you live righteously.[16]

The *Todah* Meal

One of the liturgical "ancestors" of the Mass is the *todah* of ancient Israel. It was a communion sacrifice offered to the Lord in praise and thanks for his deliverance from affliction (Lev 7:12-15). Both the liturgies of the *todah* and the Eucharist give worship of God through word and meal, and an offering of bread and wine. A *todah* song begins by recalling some mortal threat that has come upon the people, but then praises God for his deliverance. The word *todah* was translated in the Septuagint as "sacrifice of praise". This term made its way into the first Eucharistic Prayer, and sums up much of what Eucharist really is. The Eucharist is a "sacrifice of praise" because it is a proclamation of the wonderful works of God within a sacrificial meal. We praise him for what he has done for us in the mystery of Jesus, the sacrificed Lamb of God.

The classic example of a *todah* is Psalm 22, which Jesus quotes in his agony on the cross, beginning with the words, "My God, my God, why have you abandoned me?" Those at the foot of the cross would have recognised this song which begins with a cry of dereliction and affliction, but ends with an exultant note of salvation and deliverance. The Psalm expresses a profound truth of Israel's covenant experience.

No matter what miserable afflictions we are enduring, we can offer them to God in confident trust, and in God's time we will find ourselves praising God in joy because he has delivered us. All who join together in the *todah*, the sacrificial meal of praise and thanksgiving, are experiencing their own poverty and affliction. They eat this meal with praise even though they are still waiting upon the saving power of the Lord, who will free them from their trials and tribulations.

They may not yet see any answers to their problems, but they still praise God. This is our Eucharistic attitude. "The afflicted shall eat and be satisfied, those who seek him shall praise the Lord" (Ps 22:26). Based on our memory of the Lord's faithfulness to his covenant, we come now with all our struggles, sorrows and adversities, and we praise him with joy. We do so because we know he delivers us. Jesus' resurrection from death is our deliverance. It is a sign and pledge of our freedom. All the afflicted who trust in the Lord are invited to celebrate the Christian *todah*, the Eucharist, the sacrificial meal of praise. This meal is full of promise. It is the pledge of the coming wedding feast of the Lamb with his bride the Church. "The poor shall eat and shall have their fill. They who seek the Lord shall praise him. May their hearts live forever and ever." (Ps 22:27)

The Gift of Praise

Strangely enough, even though the Eucharist is all about praising God, many are still shy about this dimension of the Church's prayer. Sometimes the Sunday celebration is but a miserable murmur of solemn assembly rather than a people joyfully praising God for his wonderful goodness and love. Recently Pope Francis, reflecting on David joyfully dancing before the Ark of the Covenant, warned us that "if we close ourselves in formality, our prayer becomes cold and sterile." He continued, "David's prayer of praise brought him to let go of normal composure and to dance in front of the Lord with all his strength. This is the prayer of praise!"[17] He noted that we are good at asking God for things, and even thanking him. But the prayer of praise is forgotten. He said some people may object that this prayer of praise is for the charismatic renewal not for everyone. "No" he said, "the prayer of praise is a Christian prayer for all of us! ... In Mass, every day, when we sing the *Holy, Holy, Holy*, this is the prayer of praise: we praise God for his greatness, because he is great!" The Pope went on to encourage us all to sing the *Gloria* and the *Holy, Holy, Holy* not only with the mouth, but with the heart. He pointed out that Michal was rendered sterile because she ridiculed David's spontaneous praise of God. And he warned that if we shut ourselves up in "cold, measured prayer" we may well end up like Michal, spiritually sterile (2 Sam 6:12-23).

The word Eucharist comes from the Greek word *"eucharistein"* meaning thanksgiving. It is the Church giving thanks for the good gift (*eu-charis*) of God in his creation and redemption. We remember his goodness, displayed especially in the redemption won for us by Jesus through his death and resurrection. At the Last Supper Jesus took the bread and prayed a *berakah* prayer, a Hebrew blessing prayer, and then pronounced the words of institution. The Eucharistic prayer is modelled on the *berakah* prayers, which bless God for all he has done to save and deliver us. A Eucharistic outlook fosters an "attitude of gratitude" in us as God's people. We remember the "mirabilia Dei", the wonderful works of God, especially in God taking on our humanity, Jesus broken in his passion, shedding his blood for us, and now risen and glorified. But our thanksgiving gives rise to praise. We praise God for who he is in all his splendour, beauty, and majesty. We exalt him for his tender mercy, kindness and infinite goodness of heart. We join the angels and saints in heaven in the eternal song of praise around the throne of the Lamb, "Amen. Praise and glory and wisdom and thanksgiving and honour and power and strength to our God for ever and ever. Amen." (Rev 7:13)

Augustine on Praise

There was nothing shy about St Augustine in calling his liturgical assemblies to praise God:

> We offer up a sacrifice of gladness, a sacrifice of rejoicing, a sacrifice of thanksgiving, which no words can express. But where do we offer it? In his own tabernacle, that is, in the holy Church. And what is the sacrifice we offer? An overflowing and ineffable joy, beyond words, not to be expressed in speech. Such is the sacrifice of jubilation.[18]

He is calling here for "jubilation", a spontaneous surge of sound from the congregation which would be beyond words, but would express the heart of worship. This is a way of allowing the love of God to overflow in wordless sounds. He describes how it arises:

> Before you experienced God in love, you thought that you could express God in words. You begin to experience him in the union of love, and at once you cannot express what you experience. But ... will you be mute, will you not praise God? You praised him when you were seeking him, will you be silent when you have found him? By no means! It is then that the jubilation which is fully worthy of the name bursts forth![19]

Jubilation certainly burst forth in the liturgical assemblies in Hippo. During the Easter Eucharist a young man named Paulus was completely healed of a disease, and stood before the congregation. "Everyone", says Augustine, "burst into a prayer of thankfulness to God. The whole church soon rang with the clamour of rejoicing ... In the crowded church, cries of joy rose up everywhere, 'Thanks be to God' 'Praise be to God' with everyone joining and shouting on all sides ... and still with louder voices shouting again." The next day the young man's sister was healed of the same disease. He says "the tumult of joy" burst forth like a roar:

Such wonder rose from men and women together that the exclamations and the tears seemed as if they would never come to an end ... They shouted God's praises without words, but with such a noise that our ears could scarcely bear it."[20]

The Church's Worship

The subjective disposition of the individuals worshipping will determine the quality of the worship. However, we must remember that the Eucharist is the supreme act of the divine liturgy, which by definition is the *public worship of the Church*. In the liturgy the Church shares in the priestly worship of Christ. "In it full public worship is performed by the mystical body of Jesus Christ, that is, by the Head and the members."[21] In the liturgy we participate in Christ's own prayer to the Father, through the Holy Spirit, which is always efficacious. The Doxology at the end of the Eucharistic Prayer sums this up beautifully, "Through him (Christ), and with him, and in him, O God Almighty Father, in the unity of the Holy Spirit, all glory and honour is yours, forever and ever. Amen."

The Eucharist, like all liturgical worship, is the work of the Trinity. We are celebrating the life of the Father, Son and Spirit which we already possess through Baptism, and we are deepened more in this baptismal identity. The prayers of the Eucharist, like all liturgical prayer, are almost always addressing the Father. "The Father is acknowledged and adored as the source and end of all the blessings of creation and salvation."[22] All liturgy is a response of adoration, praise and thanksgiving, whereby we, the Church, "bless" the Father for every good gift. The Eucharist is the highest moment of this whole-hearted response of the Church to the Father's faithful love.

Without Christ our worship would be useless, nothing better than the futile efforts of the ancient people building the tower of Babel (Gen 11:1-9). By using our own imagination, ingenuity and will-power, we would be trying to reach heaven in vain. But in liturgy Christ changes our worship into his own. He has taken over our worship since he is the one true mediator who can bridge the gap between earth and heaven. He is the only one who can offer to the Father a worship that is truly pleasing in his sight. Through the action of Christ in the Eucharist our worship is changed into the great mystery of the worship which Christ offered on Calvary. The Eucharist makes present the dying and rising of Jesus, the paschal mystery, which occurred once in history, but is now eternal because Christ is glorified. The Eucharist, as we shall see, re-presents the sacrifice of Jesus on the cross and makes available the full power of his resurrection. This also means that our offerings of bread and wine do not remain simply symbols of our lives. They are changed into that which he offered on the cross, his own body and blood.

The Eucharist is also the action of the Holy Spirit. The Church exists because of the Holy Spirit. In Eucharist, we gather and we worship in the communion of the Holy Spirit. The Holy Spirit unites our offering today with that of Christ over two thousand years ago; and he helps us have the same heart as Jesus when he made that self-offering to the Father out of love for us. We invoke the power of the Holy Spirit upon the bread and wine before the consecration, and also upon the people gathered after the consecration. The first invocation is praying for the change of the elements into the body and blood of Christ, the second is that we will become more united as Church, which is the ultimate purpose of our receiving the real presence of Jesus.

PART II
SACRIFICE

The Mass makes present the sacrifice of the cross; it does not add to that sacrifice nor does it multiply it. What is repeated is its memorial celebration, its 'commemorative re-presentation', which makes Christ's one, redemptive sacrifice always present in time. (Pope John Paul II)

Harshly dealt with, he bore it humbly, he never opened his mouth, like a lamb that is lead to the slaughter-house, like a sheep that is dumb before its shearers never opening its mouth. (Isaiah 53:7)

4

THE LAST SUPPER

"The life I now live in this body I live in faith; faith in the Son of God who loved me and who sacrificed himself for my sake." (Gal 2:21)

Sacrament of Love

At the Last Supper Jesus opened his heart to his disciples, "I have longed with a great longing to eat this Passover with you before I suffer" (Lk 22:15). This love in the heart of Jesus was burning for us all, desiring to sacrifice himself on our behalf. Earlier in Luke's gospel he had cried out "I have come to bring fire to the earth and how I wish it were blazing already" (Lk 12:49). He was speaking of the fire of love within his heart for all humanity, which was driving him forward to sacrifice himself on the cross. He continued, "There is a baptism I must undergo and how greatly I am constrained until it is accomplished". This "baptism" was the immersion into suffering which he was longing to endure out of love for us. Jesus took the bread, said the blessing prayer, broke the bread, and gave it to them saying, "This is my body which will be *given up* for you" (Lk 22:19). He was speaking prophetically of what was to happen the following day; a word in action which anticipated, and brought about, what it proclaimed. The motivation for his sacrifice was his immense love.

John's account of the Last Supper begins with the reminder that it was the eve of the Passover, and "Jesus knew *the hour* had come for him to pass from this world to the Father" (Jn 13:1). This *hour* for which he had longed was the *hour* of his passion and death for our sake. It was the *hour* when he would prove to us his love. "Having loved his own in the world he loved them to the end." This is a love which knows no measure. The heart of Jesus was full to overflowing with sacrificial love for each one of us, a love which would take him to the cross. As Paul says, "What proves that God loves us that Christ died for us while we were still sinners" (Rom 5:8). The Last Supper already anticipated prophetically the love offering of Jesus to the Father in his passion and death on the following day.

This longing of Christ to give himself completely for our sake was in perfect cooperation with the Father's will. The heart of the Father also was totally and unconditionally committed to our redemption: "God so loved the world that he gave his only Son, so that everyone who believes in him may not be lost but may have eternal life." (Jn 3:16) During the passion and agonising death of Jesus on the cross the Father was not impassive and indifferent. He was suffering *with* Jesus. He gave over his Son as a gift of love for us. As Paul says, "Since God did not spare his only Son, but gave him up for us all, we can be certain, after such a gift, that he would not refuse anything he can give" (Rom 8:32). The Eucharist is a sacrament of this wonderful sacrificial love of God, his total self-giving love on our behalf. What could have motivated God to be sentenced to death as a criminal and crucified between two criminals with such disgrace, shame and dishonour to his divine Majesty? St Bernard asks, "Who has done this?" He gives the answer, "Love has done it – love that is forgetful of dignity."

Jesus: The New Paschal Lamb

In the gospels Jesus chose to celebrate the Last Supper in the context of the Jewish Passover meal. This meal was a memorial celebration of the Exodus – the liberation of the people from slavery in Egypt and entry into the promised land (Ex 12:26-27). In the ritual which was a memorial of the saving act of God, rescuing his people from slavery, the people actually relived these events. By the way they dressed, the food they ate, and the prayers that were offered, they sought to recreate the experience of the Exodus. The celebration itself made these liberating events present and active now. A key symbol was the Passover lamb which had to be slain and eaten, but not a bone was to be broken. Some of the blood of the lamb was to be put on the doorposts of the Israelites to protect them from the destruction that was to come.

At the time of Jesus the Jewish Passover consisted of the sacrificing of the lambs in the Temple in the afternoon of the 14 Nisan, and then the eating of the victim during the Passover supper in family homes on the following night. During the meal the head of the family would tell the story of God's wonderful saving deeds, and also explain the meaning of the symbols of the meal.

John's gospel gives primary focus upon the sacrifice in the Temple at 3pm on the day before the Passover celebration. Early in the gospel Jesus is identified by John the Baptist, "Behold the Lamb of God, who takes away the sin of the world" (Jn 1:29). Jesus dies on Calvary at the very time that the lambs of the old Passover are being immolated in the Temple. Jesus is the new paschal Lamb. When he was sacrificed on the cross, his body is likened to the paschal lamb of old, since we are told "not a bone was broken". (Jn 19:36)

The Synoptic gospel writers chose to focus on the family meal in the evening and place the Last Supper in this setting. For them the Eucharist was instituted when the Passover meal was being celebrated. Jesus was the new paschal Lamb being eaten. What happened during the meal was a prophetic sign of the sacrifice on Calvary which was to take place the next day. The ritual was a concrete realisation of God's word, and anticipated what was to come. Both the approach of the Synoptics and that of John are rich in meaning and both complement one another. The question about the historical timing of the Last Supper and the death of Jesus is relatively unimportant. Whatever about the timing of events, we can have no doubt from the New Testament evidence that the Eucharist is a memorial of the new Passover of Christ to the Father which took place on the cross, and was anticipated in the Last Supper meal. As Paul exclaimed, "Christ, our paschal lamb, has been sacrificed!" (1 Cor 5:7)

Memorial Meal of the New Covenant

In the accounts of the Last Supper given by Mathew and Mark Jesus takes the cup and says, "This is my blood, the blood of the covenant, which will be poured out for the many for the forgiveness of sins" (Mt 26:28). Again this is a prophetic action speaking of his death. The language evokes the memory of the rather graphic sealing of the old covenant by Moses with the sprinkling of the blood of bullocks. Moses had received the commandments on Mt Sinai, and written them down, since they expressed the love response expected by the people to God's faithful love of them. The promise of God had been "I will be your God and you shall be my people." It was time for Moses and the people to ritually ratify the covenant. He built an altar at the foot of the mountain. They then offered holocausts and immolated bullocks. Moses cast half the blood on the altar. Then he read the written Covenant to the listening people. They all responded that they would obey all that the Lord had decreed. Then Moses, carrying the rest of the blood in basins, sprinkled it upon the people. The words he spoke as he did this are telling, "This is the blood of the covenant that the Lord has made with you in accordance with all these words of his" (Ex 24:8). After this the people shared a meal together.

All of this symbolism comes into play at the Last Supper. The words of Jesus pick up on the words of Moses and show that what was happening now was the sealing of the *new* covenant, not in the blood of bullocks, but in his *own* blood. The words of institution in the liturgy of the Eucharist today spell it out clearly, "This is the chalice of *my* blood, the blood of the *new and eternal* covenant." Clearly at the Last Supper Jesus, in prophetic action, was speaking of his death on the cross as a sacrifice for all, a self-giving offering for the sake of all men and women. Through these words he was already making present sacramentally the once for all sacrifice of Calvary, the shedding of his blood. This was the sealing of God's utterly faithful covenantal love for us, and the paying of the price for our redemption. "You know that you were ransomed from the futile ways you had inherited from your ancestors, not with perishable things like silver and gold, but with the precious blood of Christ, like that of a lamb without defect or blemish." (1 Pet 18-19)

5

CHRIST: BROKEN AND GIVEN

"This is the love I mean: not our love for God, but God's love for us when he sent his Son to be the sacrifice that takes our sins away." (1 Jn 4:10)

The Heart of Jesus, broken open in Love

Eucharist is not foremost what we do for God, rather it is a celebration of what God has done for us. We remember God's tender mercy and faithfulness, and proclaim with all our hearts that "his steadfast love endures forever". This love and mercy of our God has been revealed in a definitive way in his passion and death on the cross. In Eucharist we gaze upon Jesus crucified, caught up in the immensity of his sacrifice for our sake. Our eyes are opened in wonder to the overwhelming gift of his love. As Paul says, "The love of Christ overwhelms us when we think that one man died when we all should have died, but he died so that living men should live no longer for themselves, but for him who died and was raised to life for them" (2 Cor 5:14-15). This explosive love in the heart of Christ for the world is made present for us in Eucharist. By participating in Eucharist we are opened up more deeply to the experience of this love. We find his love more and more persuasive, to the point of being compelling. We are saturated with his love and become convinced of how radically committed he is towards us. The craziness of his love for us creates in our hearts a "divine madness". Our only response can be to give all to him in return.

The whole revelation of God's love is contained in a mysterious way in the pierced heart of Christ on the cross. Contemplating this mystery is the starting point for appreciating the depths of his love for us. Pope Benedict says, "It is there that our definition of love must begin."[23] We experience the divine love in the human heart of Jesus. John's gospel tells us that the soldier pierced the side of Christ with a lance, from which flowed blood and water. This was to fulfil the prophecy, "They shall look upon him whom they have pierced" (Jn 19:37). How true this prophecy has been in the history of the Church and how true it is for us today as well! The death of Jesus on the cross is the culmination of the story of God's love in its most radical form, whereby the Father gave over his Son for the sake of the world, and the Son gave over himself to the Father for our sake. We joyfully proclaim the death of the Lord until he comes again:

> Through the mystery of his wounded heart, the restorative tide of God's merciful love continues to spread over the men and women of our time. Here alone can those who long for true and lasting happiness find its secret.[24]

This font from his side had been predicted by Jesus earlier when he had cried out on the last day of the festival, "Let anyone who is thirsty come to me, and let the one who believes in me drink. As scripture says, from his breast shall flow fountains of living water." John tells us, "He was speaking of the Spirit which those who believed him were to receive; for there was no Spirit yet because Jesus had not yet been glorified." (Jn 7:17-19)

In the early Church the water flowing from the side of Christ became an image of the Spirit being poured out to bring new life. The blood spoke of his mercy, the price he was prepared to pay for our redemption, given for us until the last drop was shed. This imagery was seen to apply to Baptism and Eucharist. The Fathers remembered how Eve was brought into being from the side of Adam. Now the Church, the new Eve, was birthed mysteriously from the side of Christ on the cross, the new Adam. So the whole sacramental life of the Church, especially the Eucharist, was seen to be birthed from wounded side of Jesus.

The Eucharist makes present Christ's redeeming sacrifice, the power of infinite unconditional love that transforms human hearts and makes us one. This is the wonderful self-gift of Christ to his Bride, the Church. On the Cross from the wounded side of Christ the Church was born. Now in the Eucharist, the power of Christ's self-giving love is made present and active for us. This gives the Church life. As Mother Teresa once said, "When we look at the crucifix we know how Jesus loved us *then*. When we receive him in the Eucharist we know how he loves us *now*." Whenever we are celebrating Eucharist we are remembering this immense love of Jesus, we are hungering for him, and are seeking to radically open ourselves up to receive more of his love.

Having received such selfless love our hearts are so enflamed that we can give no other response than to offer our lives to God in love without reserve. We enter fully into his perfect sacrifice to the Father, and his self-giving love for the world.

Sacrament of the Sacrifice of Christ

We believe that "The sacrifice of Christ and the sacrifice of the Eucharist are one single sacrifice."[25] But *how* is the Eucharist the sacrifice of Christ? This question has been a point of contention between Catholics and Protestants since the Reformation. Before proceeding to reflect on the significance of the Eucharistic sacrifice we need to discuss briefly this theological question.

To avoid any misunderstanding it is important to stress that

Catholics do not believe that we are repeating the sacrifice of Jesus on the cross, as if there is anything we could add to its efficacy for our salvation. Before breathing his last on the cross Jesus cried out, "It is finished!" (Jn 19:30). This means all that needed to happen for our redemption has been accomplished. In Hebrews we find also a strong affirmation that Jesus' perfect offering to the Father on the cross was once and for all effective for our salvation. His sacrifice of self-giving love in obedience to the Father was all-sufficient in atoning for the sin of humankind:

> He does not have to offer himself again and again, like the high priest going into the sanctuary year after year with the blood that is not his own ... he has made his appearance once and for all, now at the end of time, to do away with sin by sacrificing himself. (Heb 9:25-26)

St Augustine taught that the Eucharist *renews* the event of Calvary by *celebrating* it (not repeating it). Following Augustine, contemporary theologians like to use the idea of "sacrament" to help understand this. A sacrament "signifies what it effects and effects what it signifies". So the Eucharist is an efficacious sign of the once for all sacrifice of Jesus. This is a way of stressing that the Eucharist does not repeat Calvary, but it *re-presents* the event, or makes it present here and now. In the Eucharist, as a worshipping people, we join with Jesus in his perfect prayer to the Father. Our liturgical action is the means by which the great sacrifice of Jesus is made present and the fruits of this sacrifice are made fully available to us.[26]

Other theologians use the idea of "memory", or in Greek "anamnesis", to explain this identity of Calvary and the Eucharistic sacrifice. This way of remembering is not as a photo, or a monument, or a day of remembrance may evoke recollection of a significant event of the past. It is a rich concept based on the way the Israelites celebrated the memory of the Exodus. The memorial ritual meal of the Passover was understood to make present and active the events of the Exodus in the lives of participants. Those celebrating the past events experienced *now* the liberating, saving power of God manifest in those events. They experienced the events again and again and hence they benefitted more and more from their liberating effect. In fact the celebration of these foundational events in their history deepened them in their fundamental identity, confirming them more as the people of God.

In a similar way, Jesus instructed us to "Do this in memory of me." Whenever we celebrate this memorial meal, the events of the saving death and resurrection of Jesus are made present and operative in our lives. The Eucharist is a memorial meal of the once for all sacrifice of Jesus, his great Exodus to the Father, which broke the power of sin and death. In the act of remembering we are drawn into, and participate in, the death and resurrection of Jesus. In the liturgy of the Passover meal at the time of Jesus, the Jews used to say, "In every generation, let each one see himself as the one who came out of Egypt that night."[27] We as Christians, celebrating the new Passover meal, may say that in every generation each of us in the Eucharist sees himself or herself standing beneath the cross the day Jesus died, united with Mary and John in the community of disciples. The famous Negro spiritual asks the question, "Were you there when they crucified my Lord?" Our answer is "Yes, I was there!" And we can say together as the worshipping people of God, "Yes, *we* were there!" In Eucharistic liturgy, as we remember and relive the great events of Easter and Pentecost, which birthed the Church, we are deepened in our identity as the *new* people of God, and empowered to grow more in who we are meant to be.

These theological explanations all have merit, but ultimately we are left in mystery. There is also another way by which we can understand the perpetuation of the power of the cross down through the centuries, and its continuing effect in our lives. I am referring to the Holy Spirit! The Eucharist is made possible by the Spirit living in the Church. There is a sense in which we can say that the work of the cross is a work of the Holy Spirit. In the Mass before the priest consumes the sacred host, he prays to Jesus, "through the will of the Father, and the *work of the Holy Spirit*, your death brought life to the world". It was the Holy Spirit, who is the love between the Father and Son from all eternity, who inspired Jesus with the fire in his heart to long to offer himself to the Father for us. It was the Holy Spirit who led him to the cross, and it was the Holy Spirit who Jesus breathed upon the world when he expired on the cross (*cf*. Lk 23:46). It was the Holy Spirit who breathed on the dead body of Jesus in the tomb and brought him to life (Rom 8:11). It is the Holy Spirit in the celebration of Eucharist who enables us to actually experience Calvary now, and to encounter the risen Christ. In the Eucharistic celebration there are two invocations of the Holy Spirit, one to call upon the Spirit to effect the consecration, and one to call upon the Holy Spirit to unite us in Christ through communion. The Holy Spirit brings the power of the cross into our personal lives when we allow him to work within us; and the Holy Spirit also makes the cross effective for us in the liturgy of the Eucharist.

"My body given up for you"

Because the Eucharist re-presents the sacrifice of Jesus for us, it is a moment when we respond wholeheartedly to his love. We are drawn to express and deepen our *surrender* to the Father's love. If we are fully and consciously participating in the celebration we allow ourselves to be drawn into the love between Jesus and the Father by the action of the Holy Spirit. We intentionally offer ourselves with the perfect offering of Jesus to the Father. We lay our *whole lives* on the altar as a response of love to the overwhelming love of God who has redeemed us by the precious blood of Jesus. At the Last Supper, Jesus said "this is my body which will be *given up* for you" and "this is my blood...which will be *poured out* for many". Then he said, "Do this in memory of me". He was inviting us not only to repeat the ritual again, and to benefit from its immense graces, but also *to do the essence of what he has done*. What has he done? He has offered himself; *given up* and *poured out* for our sake. He has offered his whole life as a loving sacrifice to the Father; an act of perfect love. We are invited to join him in this self-offering; that is, to offer ourselves as a living sacrifice to the Father with him.

We are reminded again of the text from Romans, "Think of God's mercy, my brothers, and worship him, I beg you, in a way that his worthy of thinking beings, by offering your living bodies as a holy sacrifice, truly pleasing to God" (Rom 12:1). The word "body" here means the gift of one's whole life – all the joys and triumphs, the struggles and hardships, the whole of one's earthly existence – to be given up in union with the perfect offering of Jesus on the cross. We want our whole lives to be a love gift to the Father in and through the one perfect act of love expressed in the sacrifice of Jesus. So when we are participating in the celebration of the Eucharist we can bring our poor lives in their raw reality – all the confusion, struggle, brokenness, as well as all the triumphs and joys – our whole personal existence- and present it all with Jesus to the Father. The movement of our hearts is to give ourselves over, in union with the perfect self-giving of Jesus, to the Father.

"Body broken for you"

We have already seen how the early Christians' favourite term for the Eucharist was "the breaking of the bread". This central ritual action in the celebration was not only a symbol of fraternal sharing. It carried a more profound meaning. The "breaking" spoke of an act of immolation, a *sacrificial* meaning. In breaking the bread at the Last Supper Jesus was expressing that he himself was being "broken" before the Father for our sake. The famous servant song of Isaiah refers to Jesus: "He was broken for our transgression, crushed for our sins. On him lies a punishment that brings us peace, and through his wounds we are healed" (Is 55:5). Jesus, in breaking the bread at the Last Supper, was in reality "breaking" himself before the Father. The essence of the sacrifice of Jesus to the Father was his obedience, his will given over completely to the Father's will in total trust, in the midst of the darkness of our sin which had been laid upon him. So Jesus, a human being like us in all things but sin, "breaks himself" before the Father for our sake. This action speaks of his human will being "broken" in obedience to the Father. The mystery of our redemption was essentially this breaking of himself, totally given to the Father for our sake. The first key moment was in the Garden of Gethsemane, when in a paroxysm of fear, he uttered, "Father, if it be possible take this cup from me, but your will not mine be done." The second key moment was his surrender on the cross, "Father into your hands I commit my spirit."

In Hebrews the author, speaking of the offering of Jesus, quotes psalm 40, "You have not desired sacrifices and offerings … but a body you have prepared for me … See, I have come to do your will, O God" (Heb 10:5). The author is keen to point out that the old mode of sacrifice, using bulls and goats, was no longer desired by God. Rather the Father was asking for a new mode of sacrifice, the surrender of human will to God's will. This is the heart of the sacrifice of Jesus to the Father, which we can share in Eucharist. Surrendering our lives to God is not easy. We need to overcome any resistance within us. The deepest sickness of the human heart is rebellion against God, a refusal to worship him and give him glory. Jesus, in solidarity with us, has turned this around. As Paul puts it succinctly, "As by one man's disobedience many were made sinners, so by one man's obedience many will be made righteous." (Rom 5:19)

The Eucharist is now the privileged place where we can join with Jesus in this liberating movement of heart, mind, soul and body – to do what Jesus did that evening in the upper room, to "break" ourselves, and lay ourselves totally before God. It is fundamentally a *breaking of one's will* before God, a laying of our will on the altar with Jesus, but not only the will but one's whole self and all that makes up one's life. All the hardness of heart, rebelliousness of spirit and prideful resistance must be crushed, as we say a deep "yes" in surrender to God. The Sequence prayer in the Pentecost liturgy has that heartfelt plea for the work of the Holy Spirit, "Bend the stubborn heart and will, melt the frozen, warm the chill." That is what we ask for as we enter into Eucharist, that we shall yield more deeply to the will of God in our lives, that our stubbornness will be truly broken with the breaking of the bread, that our hearts shall be set on fire, and that our lives shall be truly sacrificial in union with Jesus.

6

SELF-GIVING LOVE FOR US

"Try then to imitate God, as children of his that he loves, and follow Christ by loving as he loved you, giving himself up in our place as a fragrant offering and a sacrifice to God." (Eph 5:1-2)

The Church's Offering

We have seen how the essence of the sacrifice of Jesus to the Father offered on the cross was his self-giving love and surrender to the Father's will. So in the Eucharist we are drawn into this same fire of love that was in the heart of Jesus, and we are able to surrender our hearts in obedience to the Father in and through his perfect offering. Our participation in Eucharist becomes more heightened in intensity the more we purposefully unite ourselves with the sacrifice of Jesus.

In the Eucharist the Church offers herself and is offered at the same time. Each of the members of the Church is involved in this wonderful dynamic. It is not the priest alone who offers the sacrifice, while the rest of the faithful remain passive and uninvolved. All the faithful are both priest and victim. Of course, only the ordained priest acts in the person of Christ as Head when he takes the bread and wine, prays the blessing prayer, breaks the bread and gives. But, the whole Church and each of its members, as the priesthood of the faithful through baptism, offer ourselves together with the perfect offering of Jesus. He is the Head, we are the body, being offered together:

> The Church which is the body of Christ participates in the offering of her Head. With him, she herself is offered whole and entire. She unites herself to his intercession with the Father for all men. In the Eucharist the sacrifice of Christ becomes also the sacrifice of the members of his body. The lives of the faithful, their praise, sufferings, prayer, and work, are united with those of Christ and with his total offering, and so acquire a new value. Christ's sacrifice present on the altar makes it possible for all generations of Christians to be united with his suffering.[28]

Here is a key to the heart of Eucharistic worship – that we offer ourselves to God in union with the perfect sacrifice of Jesus. We bring our whole lives with all the pain and struggle, as well as the joys and triumphs, and give ourselves unreservedly into the hands of the loving Father.

This act of love on our part can only happen because Christ has first loved us. We are not the ones who take the initiative, as if we come to Eucharist to win God's favour. No! Our worship is a response to what God has done in Christ to redeem us. The Eucharist is primarily a gift of God's saving love for us. In the Eucharist we gaze upon the pierced side of Jesus on the cross from which flowed blood and water for our salvation. Jesus gave enduring presence to this act of oblation when he instituted the Eucharist. By participating in the Eucharist we firstly *receive* this immense love given to us so lavishly by Jesus on the cross, and then we *respond* to him by sharing in this self-giving love. With Jesus we surrender totally to the Father and allow our hearts to expand in love with Jesus for all men and women.

Surrender all to God

Being caught up in the love that Christ has for us we want to *give all* in return. Eucharist has a way of drawing us out of our self-centred attitudes and loosening us from unruly desires and inordinate attachments. The grace of Eucharist empowers us to become more fully human by making us less self-centred and more given for others. We desire more to empty ourselves of all our useless attachments and seek God alone. We let the Lord's love possess us, so that we are willing to give over to him the areas of our lives where we are still in control. By emptying ourselves we are making room for the living God to dwell more deeply within us. We join with the sacrifice of Jesus, who said of his own offering, "Unless a grain of wheat falls into the ground and dies it remains but a grain of wheat, but if it dies it yields a rich harvest" (Jn 12:24). In sacrifice there is a dying to self for a transcendent purpose. "Anyone who wants to save his life will lose it; but anyone who loses his life for my sake, and for the sake of the gospel, will save it." (Mk 8:35)

"The Eucharist draws us into Jesus' act of self-oblation. More than just statically receiving the incarnate Logos, we enter into the very dynamic of his self-giving."[29] In this regard it can be helpful at the time when the gifts are being brought up at the offertory to imagine oneself being taken forward and as it were placed on the altar. The bread and wine symbolise our lives, and all that makes up our earthly existence. We present ourselves with the gifts, so that just as they are transformed by the word spoken and the Spirit falling, we also may be changed. It can be particularly useful to give over those parts of our lives where there is some resistance, or maybe those areas where we simply need deeper transformation. This attitude of surrender and abandonment in love is real Eucharistic worship.

During the Eucharistic prayer we can continue in this sacrificial mind-set, offering ourselves with Jesus. We bring the various parts of our lives that are not yet given to the Father, and sacrifice them with

Jesus' perfect sacrifice. In this way we become more aware of how much we depend on the things of this world to make us feel good about ourselves and to give us a sense of security and meaning in our lives. We let go of these things that may be ruling our hearts and preventing us from becoming fully who we are meant to be. We come to a deeper place of surrender to the Father's will, in and through the "yes" that Jesus made to the Father in his passion and ultimately in his death on the cross.

Power for Transformation

The redeeming action of Jesus through his cross and resurrection is a transforming power which renews the world. Through the Eucharist "the 'hour' of Jesus becomes our hour".[30] The victory of love over hatred, the victory of life over death, of good conquering evil has triggered off a series of transformations that little by little will change the world. Pope Benedict likens this on-going transformation to the process of "nuclear fission in the heart of being".[31] All other attempts to change the world are limp and ultimately ineffective. The power of the redemptive act of Jesus when he hung on the cross for our sake, and then rose triumphantly from the grave, is the only force truly effective in changing the world. This is because it is the power of infinite love which is irrepressible.

The Eucharist perpetuates this powerful love which exploded into the universe through the death and resurrection of Jesus. His sacrifice of himself on the cross established the ultimate victory of love over hatred and his resurrection established the ultimate victory of life over death. Eucharist makes this reality present and active in our lives. But this primary transformation achieved by Jesus yields another transformation. In Eucharist, bread and wine, which symbolise our ordinary lives, are changed into the body and blood of Christ. But then the process of transformation gathers momentum. The body and blood of Christ are given to us in Holy Communion, so we can be transformed as well. We become the body of Christ, his own flesh and blood, for the world. The Eucharist builds the Church. But it is also the purpose of the Eucharist to "build" each one of us individually. Each one of us who receives the body and blood of Christ is meant to be transformed into the very likeness of Jesus. We are to become "other Christs". By eating of the fire of God's love we "become fire".[32]

When we consume the body and blood of Christ in Holy Communion we are drawn into the very dynamic of the sacrifice of Jesus, receiving the power to love as he has loved and to live as he has lived. We are empowered to totally dedicate ourselves sacrificially to the Father and to the Kingdom of God, and to totally sacrifice ourselves for others. We become deeply united with Jesus in Holy Communion, and this means we are willing to be deeply united with others. So in receiving Jesus in Holy Communion we are choosing to be in close relationship with all in his body. "Union with Jesus that excludes others in whom he finds his identity (the body of Christ) is not union at all".[33]

Love your Enemies

But there is still more to this chain reaction of love. In receiving Jesus in Holy Communion we are committing ourselves to love *all* men and women, even our enemies. Jesus says, "Love your enemies, do good to those who hate you" (Lk 6:27). This power of love that is like nuclear fission works within us to bring a mighty transformation. Nothing is impossible to God. A priest, who was the abbot of a monastery in Romania, had been imprisoned by the Communist regime. He had suffered extremely brutal torture, and was close to death. Thrown into the same jail cell were other political prisoners, including other priests and Protestant pastors. One day to their surprise one of the men who had been responsible for their torture was also thrown into the same cell. He had been beaten to a pulp as a result of falling out with the authorities. No one spoke to him. During the night his moans could he heard as he too was dying from his wounds. He would cry out, "Help me. I can't die, I have committed such terrible crimes!" What happened then is related by a Lutheran minister[34] who was an eye-witness to a miracle of love:

> I saw the agonised priest calling two other prisoners. And leaning on their shoulders, slowly, slowly he walked past my bed, sat on the bedside of this murderer, and caressed his head – I will never forget this gesture. I watched a murdered man caressing his murderer! That is love – he found a caress for him.

The priest said to the man, "You are young; you did not know what you were doing. I love you with all my heart." But he did not just *say* the words. You can say "love," and it's just a word of four letters. But he really *loved*. "I love you with all my heart."

Then he went on, "If I who am a sinner can love you so much, imagine Christ, who is Love Incarnate, how much He loves you! And all the Christians whom you have tortured, know that they forgive you, they love you, and Christ loves you. He wishes you to be saved much more than you wish to be saved. You wonder if your sins can be forgiven. He wishes to forgive your sins more than you wish your sins to be forgiven. He desires for you to be with him in heaven much more than you wish to be in heaven with him. He is Love. You only need to turn to him and repent."

In this prison cell in which there was no possibility of privacy, I overheard the confession of the murderer to the murdered. Life is more thrilling than a novel – no novelist has ever written such a thing. The murdered – near to death – received the confession of the murderer. The murdered gave absolution to his murderer.

They prayed together, embraced each other and the priest went back to his bed. Both men died that same night. It was a Christmas Eve. But it was not a Christmas Eve in which we simply remembered that two thousand years ago Jesus was born in Bethlehem. It was a Christmas Eve during which Jesus was born in the heart of a Communist murderer."

When we are cooperating with the grace of Eucharist there is no limit to the power of change in our lives. Every Eucharist celebrated sincerely and earnestly by God's people creates a chain reaction of love. We ourselves are made new by the power of love. We cannot contain this love to ourselves, but must go forth joyfully touching the suffering flesh of others and inviting them into this love. As we become more genuinely centred in the Eucharist we become more a Church ready to cross new boundaries in reaching out to others, and ready to be an instrument of reconciliation. We must overcome the odd so-called "sacristy mentality" which suggests that to be Eucharistic means to be preoccupied with the externals, forever dressing up the liturgical niceties, over concerned with the accuracy of the rubrics, and living for the "bells and smells". The Eucharist itself speaks of a far more dynamic reality, which engages us in the world, calls us to be ministers of Christ's self-giving love to others, not being selective about who we befriend, and always ready to go beyond our ecclesiastical comfort zone in search of the lost.

7

DRINKING THE CUP

"All I want is to know Christ and the power of his resurrection, and to share his sufferings by reproducing the pattern of his death." (Phil 3:10)

Can you drink the cup?
In Mark's gospel James and John, the sons of Zebedee, approached Jesus with a favour, "Allow us to sit one at your right hand and the other at your left in your glory" (Mk 10:15-46). They were after the "glory" stakes. They had missed what Jesus meant when he had just told them they were going with him to Jerusalem, and he would be brought before the chief priests and the scribes. He would be condemned to death, handed over to the pagans, and be mocked, spat upon and scourged, and then finally put to death. To be followers of Jesus meant that they would share in his suffering. Peter had earlier tried to dissuade Jesus from this sort of outrageous talk; only to be rebuked by Jesus, "Get behind me Satan, for the way you think is not God's way but man's" (Mk 8:33). The disciples were taking a long time to realise that Jesus was serious when he had said to them, "If anyone wants to be a follower of mine, let him renounce himself and take up his cross and follow me" (Mk 8:34). Jesus was preparing them for the worst, but they were still caught up in earthly glory that the messiah was expected to bring. Jesus was rewriting the script, and they were confused and resistant to it.

No doubt Jesus was a little bemused by this ingenuous request of James and John. But he put to them the question that he puts to anyone who purports to be his disciple, "Can you drink of the cup of which I am to drink?" Every time we celebrate Eucharist, even if we don't have the chance of actually drinking from the chalice, Jesus asks this question of each one of us. Genuine disciples are those who will be ready to die with him. Ultimately to drink of the cup is be in communion with Jesus' sacrifice to the Father. Paul says, "The blessing cup which we bless is a communion with the blood of Christ" (1 Cor 10:16). This not only means having fellowship with one another. The context of the passage indicates that to share the cup means to participate in the sacrifice of Christ and to have *fellowship with his sufferings*. We are meant to "reproduce the pattern of his death" every day.

When Jesus met Peter on the shores of the lake of Galilee after the resurrection, he did not reproach Peter for his desertion and miserable failures. He asked him one question, "Do you love me?" Peter, knowing the sheer mercy of Christ which he did not deserve, was able to reply unconditionally, "Lord, you know everything, you know I love you." Three times the question was put; three times the answer given, making up for Peter's triple denial. Jesus knew he now had his man; he now had someone to whom he could entrust his sheep. He says, "Feed my sheep". But then Jesus spells out what this radical discipleship will mean:

> Very truly, I tell you, when you were younger, you used to fasten your own belt and to go wherever you wished. But when you grow old you will stretch out your hands, and someone else will fasten a belt around you and take you where you do not wish to go. (Jn 21:18)

John tells us Jesus was indicating the kind of death by which Peter would give glory to God. This gospel vignette sums up the radical nature of the call to be disciples. It is all or nothing. Every time we celebrate Eucharist we are stating by our participation that we too want to be broken with Jesus on the cross, we too want our blood to be shed with his for the salvation of the world. The early Christians imbibed this truth. To "drink of the cup" in Eucharist was to prepare for martyrdom, the ultimate act of imitating Jesus in his death. The account of the martyrdom of Polycarp of Smyrna, who was a disciple of John the evangelist, is written in a Eucharistic vein. They bound him to the pyre "like a ram for sacrifice; a goodly burnt offering all ready for God". Then before they set the pyre on fire, Polycarp blessed God for granting him this "hour", "that I be numbered amongst the martyrs, to share the cup of your Christ and to rise again unto life everlasting".[35] Ignatius of Antioch, a bishop in chains, on his way to be fed to the beasts in the Roman circus, saw himself as "His wheat, ground fine by the lion's teeth to be made purest bread for Christ".[36] These early witnesses knew that by their radical discipleship they would *become* Eucharist.

Witness of Love

Maximilian Kolbe, a Polish Franciscan, died imitating the self-sacrificing love of Jesus on the cross. "Greater love has no man than he lay down his life for his friends" (Jn 15:13). When, as a punishment for prisoners escaping, men were being chosen at random to be sent to the starvation bunker, one of the condemned sobbed, "Goodbye, my dear wife, goodbye my dear children, already orphans of their father". At that point the unthinkable thing happened. A prisoner stepped forward and offered to take this married man's place. It was Fr Maximilian. Just as Jesus took our place on the cross out of love for us, so Maximilian took this man's place that he may go free. Maximilian finally died in the starvation bunker by an injection of carbolic acid, since he had survived so long, making sure he had consoled and comforted all those who died before him. This was the resplendent light of Christ's love in a hell-hole of darkness. I mention it here because it tells us about the meaning of Eucharist, which Fr Maximilian used to offer frequently in secret with other prisoners. This decision of Maximilian at a critical moment of grace would not have been possible if he had not already lived a daily life of self-giving love. His life was with Jesus, lived to the glory of God and for the sake of others. When the Lord called him to join in the ultimate sacrifice of love he was ready to respond to the moment of grace.

Oscar Romero, appointed Archbishop of San Salvador in 1977, was at first reluctant to challenge the powerful elite in the El Salvadorian society, who were oppressing the poorest of the poor. But gradually the suffering of his people became so overwhelming for him that he began to speak out on their behalf. He knew that in doing this he would endanger his life He was celebrating Mass when the assassin's bullet tore through his chest. He had just finished a homily in which he had said, "May this body immolated and this blood sacrificed for humanity nourish us, so that we may give our body and blood in suffering and pain – like Christ, not for self, but to teach justice and peace to our people ..."[37] The video called *Romero* depicts the scene dramatically. At the moment he was hit by the bullet in the chest he was holding the chalice, just after the consecration. He fell to the ground and his blood was mingled with the blood of Jesus which flowed from the chalice. Oscar Romero had drunk of the cup completely. To decide to follow Jesus means that we are prepared to become Eucharist and to shed our blood with him. The question addressed to each of us as we approach Holy Communion is, "Are you willing to drink of the cup of which Jesus drank?"

At the ordination of a priest he is instructed by the bishop to "imitate what he celebrates". This exhortation is for all of us. We become bread in the hands of Christ, bread broken and given for the sake of others. We drink of the cup and allow our lives to be poured out for others. We are called to live a sacrificial life. Maybe we will not be called to martyrdom. But we have thousands of opportunities in our daily lives to prefer others to ourselves, to die to our selfish preferences and give until it hurts. The Mass has little meaning if we do not live it through offering ourselves in acts of love and service in an on-going way. At the centre of every Eucharist is the cross. St John Chrysostom remarks that coming to drink of the cup is like bringing one's own lips to the pierced side of Christ on the cross. At the time of the consecration, when the priest elevates the host and the chalice we can look upon Christ crucified. Jesus said, "When I am lifted up I will draw all to myself" (Jn 12:32). At the small elevation during the doxology at the end of the Eucharistic prayer the priest reminds the Father of the passion of Christ, the bread of his affliction and the cup of his sufferings. This is the climax of it all. We remember the love by which Christ died for us and how much it cost him to give us the Eucharist. We rededicate ourselves as disciples of Jesus, ready to embrace the cross in following him.

PART III

COMMUNION

In sacramental communion I become one with the Lord, like all the other communicants. Union with Christ is also union with all those to whom he gives himself. I cannot possess Christ just for myself; I can belong to him only in union with his own. Communion draws me out of myself towards him, and thus also towards unity with all Christians. (Pope Benedict XVI, DCE 14)

I am the vine, you are the branches. Whoever remains in me, with me in him, bears fruit in plenty; for cut off from me you can do nothing. (Jn 15:5)

8

INTIMACY WITH JESUS

"Those who eat my flesh and drink my blood abide in me, and I in them." (Jn 6:56)

Sacrifice and Communion

In the mystery of the Eucharist the offering of sacrifice and receiving communion are intrinsically united. What unites them is the self-giving love of Jesus. Sacrifice tends to emphasise the self-giving love of Jesus in offering himself *to the Father* on our behalf. Communion tends to emphasise the self-giving love of Jesus in actually giving himself *to us* to make us one with him.

Down through the centuries, both in theological reflection and in popular devotion, the pendulum has swung one way or the other. The post-Reformation church in reaction to the Protestant challenge, tended to emphasise sacrifice, somewhat to the detriment of communion. Vatican II sought to correct the balance. But after the Council, we witnessed a time of experimentation when the communion-meal aspect of the Eucharist gained ascendancy in the popular mind. Prior to the Council, Church architecture was usually in cruciform shape, with an elongated nave having transepts and the altar of sacrifice high in the sanctuary – all speaking of a transcendent movement upward in union with the sacrifice of Jesus offered by the priest. After the Council the pendulum swung towards a more circular shape with the altar more central, seeking to emphasise the horizontal dimension of communion in the body of Christ. In this search for a more communal expression, the sense of the sacred, transcendent and sacrificial meaning of the Eucharist was sometimes lost.

It is not a question of opting for one or the other, but of seeking to keep both together. Both of these essential aspects of Eucharist need to be kept in dynamic unity. What unites them is Christ giving himself; this is really what Calvary was. Christ gave himself to the Father and he gave himself to all men and women. In giving himself to the Father he gave himself to us; and in giving himself to us he gave himself to the Father. This is the one action which engages us in Eucharist. With him we give ourselves to the Father, expressed especially in the sacrificial language of the Eucharistic prayer; and with him we give ourselves for others, expressed especially in communion. Through Holy Communion we participate more deeply in the sacrifice of Jesus to the Father, and consequently we become more self-giving in love for others. We gain all the fruits of the sacrifice of Jesus for our own lives.

The Beloved Disciple

Receiving Holy Communion is a deeply personal experience. But it is also profoundly communal. I want to consider first the interior experience of union with Jesus and the personal transformation that comes from this. Then later we will look at the all important communal dimension. The intimacy is profound. We welcome Jesus into our hearts and at that moment we are more close to him than any other time on this earthly pilgrimage. It is impossible to put words on this experience of communion with Jesus. It is all his gift of love. It is a union of hearts. But our hearts can be so hardened and coarse, or maybe just complacent and indifferent. Nevertheless Jesus draws us into an abiding union with him. Jesus says, "I am the vine, you are the branches. Whoever remains in me, with me in him, bears fruit in plenty; for cut off from me you can do nothing" (Jn 15:5). We have no life without being in him. How wonderful is this communion. He offers us friendship, a gift beyond our understanding. "A man can have no greater love than to lay down his life for his friends. You are my friends, if you do what I command you. I shall not call you servants anymore, because a servant does not know his master's business; I call you friends, because I have made known to you everything I have learnt from my Father" (Jn 15:11-15). This is such an amazing gift of love. We do not deserve to be called friends. He has made us friends by giving himself for us on the cross, and giving us the grace to respond to his love by loving him in return.

Genuine love always seeks union. Jesus desired union with us so much that he not only died on the cross for us; he emptied himself even further by giving himself to us under the appearance of bread and wine. He does not want us to consider ourselves as having to earn his favour, like a slave has to the master. That would not be possible anyway. It is all a free gift of love, whereby he shares with us the secret of his love with the Father from all eternity, and draws us into communion with the Father. At the Last Supper Jesus prayed to the Father "I have made your name known to them and will continue to make it known, so that the love with which you loved me may be in them, and so that I may be in them" (Jn 17:26). How amazing is this? The very love which Jesus has received from the Father from all eternity he wants to share with us, so we actually experience this love in our hearts. How wonderful is this "heart to heart" friendship which he draws us into!

In Psalm 42 there is a text which speaks to me of this heartfelt love between my Saviour and my poor soul. The Psalmist is pining for God, like the deer yearning for running streams. Later in the psalm there is this beautiful image, "Deep is calling on deep, like the roar of mighty cataracts." From the depth of his heart of love Jesus is calling upon the depth of my weak and broken heart, and he causes a mighty torrent of love to flow within my heart which overwhelms me with its intensity. Each time we receive Holy Communion we come into this stream of grace, which is ultimately the Holy Spirit, the love between the Father and Son from all eternity, drawing us more deeply into the life of the Trinity. Who would not thirst for this wonderful gift? How much we need to prepare our hearts for this moment of communion with the Lord! We prepare to receive him with an open heart, and to spend time in intimate fellowship with the one, who is the love of our lives. We enter most deeply and fully into communion with Jesus when in all simplicity and sincerity we say to him, as Peter did, "Lord, you know I love you!" (Jn 21:16)

Thérèse of Lisieux speaks of her first Holy Communion as the consummation of a long-desired intimacy with Jesus:

> Ah! How sweet was that first kiss of Jesus? It was a kiss of *love*; I *felt* that I was *loved*, and I said: 'I love you and I give myself to you forever! There were no demands made, no struggles, no sacrifices; for a long time now Jesus and poor little Therese had *looked at* and understood each other. That day it was no longer simply a *look*, it was a fusion; they were no longer two, Therese had vanished as a drop of water is lost in the immensity of the ocean. Jesus alone remained; He was Master, the King.[38]

Therese had previously known him *to look at* in the monstrance, but now actually *receiving* him was like a "fusion". Like all the saints she is struggling to express the reality of this union. Jesus gave us the image of the vine and the branches; we are "fused" into the vine. St Cyril of Alexandria uses similar language, "As two pieces of wax fused together make one, so whoever receives Holy Communion is so united with Christ that Christ is in him and he is in Christ."[39]

Hunger in the Human Heart

The hunger for love deep in the human heart is almost ravenous. If it is not satisfied we can do crazy things, acting outside of our normal moral boundaries, often damaging ourselves and others. This deep craving to be understood and to be loved drives many into disastrously irrational decisions and ruinous relationships. From the moment Eve was consumed by unruly passion for the fruit of tree in the garden, and Adam willingly complied with her sin, human beings have been struggling to control the all consuming desire to possess and to use the other for their own gain. No wonder that Jesus offers himself to us as food that will ultimately satisfy our deepest craving: "I am the bread of life. Whoever comes to me will never be hungry, and whoever believes in me will never thirst" (Jn 6:35). Taking greedily from the tree of the knowledge of good and evil led to disorder; but now we can receive from the tree of life, the Cross of Jesus. "The bread that I shall give," says Jesus, "is my flesh, for the life of the world" (Jn 6:51). We can "taste and see that the Lord is good." (Ps 34:9)

The all-consuming fire of God's love overtakes us in Holy Communion. We receive food for the soul; not just some spiritual inspiration, consolation or revelation, but the Beloved himself. He is our food for life. Only his love ultimately satisfies the cry of our heart for intimacy. Catherine of Siena sings of this love in a beautiful prayer:

> O boundless Love!
> Just as you gave us yourself,
> wholly God and wholly man,
> so you left us all of yourself as food
> so that while we are pilgrims in this life
> we might not collapse in our weariness
> but be strengthened by you, heavenly food.
> O mercenary people! And what has your God left you?

He has left you himself, wholly God and wholly man,
hidden under the whiteness of this bread.
O fire of love!
Was it not enough to gift us with creation in your image and likeness,
and to create us anew to grace in your Son's blood
without giving yourself as food,
The whole divine being, the whole God?
What drove you?
Nothing but your love, mad with love as you are.

9

SANCTIFICATION

"God is the source of your life in Christ Jesus, who became for us our wisdom, our righteousness, our sanctification and our redemption." 1 Cor 1:30

The Fire of the Spirit

One of the lasting effects after we have received Holy Communion is a deeper indwelling of the Holy Spirit. The sacramental presence of God lasts but a short time, only until the elements disappear. But his presence through the Holy Spirit continues and grows within us. Communion is like the fire that engulfed the burning bush. The gift of Christ's body and blood feeds that fire. St Ephrem the Syrian (c. 306-373) wrote of Jesus: "He called the bread his living body, and filled it with himself and the Spirit ... He who eats it with faith eats fire and Spirit ... Take and eat this, all of you, and eat with it the Holy Spirit. For it is truly my body and whoever eats it will have eternal life."[40] The time after communion is a precious moment to be cherished. Thomas Aquinas spoke of it this way: "By the power of this sacrament the soul is spiritually nourished in that it is filled with delight in a spiritual way and, in a sense, intoxicated with the sweetness of the divine goodness, according to the Song of Songs 5:1, 'Eat my friends, and drink, and be inebriated, my dear ones'."[41]

In Communion Jesus gives us his Spirit, not as the one who gave the Spirit a long time ago, but who "gives up his Spirit" *now* (*cf.* Jn 19:30). We are immersed into the Holy Spirit's anointing of Jesus. We are inebriated with the Spirit. Paul warns us, "Do not get drunk with wine, but be filled with the Spirit" (Eph 5:18). St Ambrose says, "Holy is this inebriation which brings about sobriety of heart."[42] This spiritual intoxication is different from getting drunk on wine. When we get drunk from alcohol or drugs we "get high", and become less inhibited. In a sense we get out of ourselves, but this earthly inebriation takes us more towards the animal state, reducing our humanity. In contrast, when we are inebriated with the Spirit we get out of ourselves (the word "ecstasy" means this) and into deeper communion with God, so we can say "it is no longer I who lives, but Christ lives in me" (Gal 2:20). We become more conformed to Christ, and hence more human.

The fathers of the Church taught that the surest way to receive the Holy Spirit was by receiving the blood of Jesus in Holy Communion. If we receive the blood we receive the Spirit. The teaching is summed up by an author in the tradition of Origen, "Through the blood shed for us, we receive the Holy Spirit. The blood and the Spirit have been linked so that by the blood, which is part of our nature, we should be able to receive the Holy Spirit, which is beyond our nature."[43] To drink the blood, under the sign of wine, is to drink fire! As St Ephrem, using the words of Jesus, says, "I give you wine to drink in which fire and Spirit are mingled."[44] This way of thinking was probably influenced by the idea that blood was the life principle in the human body. But it is a profoundly biblical concept. In John's gospel, Jesus "gave up" his Spirit, and then immediately after that blood and water flowed from his side (*cf.* Jn 19:30-34). Later John was to say, "There are three witnesses, the Spirit, the water and the blood" (1 Jn 5:8). How wonderful is this immense privilege to be able to drink of the blood of Christ and so be filled to overflowing with the Holy Spirit.

The sacramental presence of the blood may quickly vanish but the on-going presence in the Holy Spirit endures. Thus, we are drawn ever more deeply into the life of the Trinity.

Changed into His Likeness

Through the fire of love given by the Holy Spirit in the Eucharist we are changed, made holy. This does not happen automatically. But when we enter into the worship in the Mass with a surrendered heart, and when we receive Holy Communion with a humble and contrite heart, we are conformed to Jesus. We receive the Beloved to become like the Beloved. The fruit of our heartfelt communion with Jesus is that we are gradually changed more and more into his likeness. This is why we need to come to Holy Communion often. The more we surrender our hearts to Jesus in love, and allow him to pour his Spirit into us, the more he can fashion in us his attitudes, his mind, his outlook, his actions. As Paul says, "For all who are in Christ Jesus there is a new creation; the old is gone and the new is here" (2 Cor 5:17). While we are already a new creation through our Baptism, the work of our sanctification is on-going and never finished. When we receive Christ in Holy Communion his transforming love is at work deeply within us. By the power of his Spirit he is changing us into the fullness of the persons we were meant to be. As we experience his presence within us and allow him to have his way with us we are "being changed into the likeness of Christ from one degree of glory to the next. This is the work of the Lord who is the Spirit." (2 Cor 4:18)

St Thérèse of Lisieux shares of a grace that she received as a young teenager after having gone to Midnight Mass at Christmas and "receiving the *strong* and *powerful* God" in Holy Communion.[45] Prior to this time she had suffered from hypersensitivity. Even small set-backs or negative comments from others would affect her deeply and bring her to tears. Having arrived home after the Mass she was subject to an insensitive comment from her tired father, which would normally have shattered her. But she testifies that she was no longer the same. At that moment she knew she had been given a new grace. Jesus had changed her heart. Instead of taking it personally and dissolving into tears she calmly met her father with love, overcoming her emotions which would normally have ruled her. She had gained a new strength of soul which she says never left her.

We Become what We Eat

Through the Eucharist we are not only sustained by what we eat. We actually *become* what we eat. St Leo the Great wrote: "Our partaking of the body and blood of Christ tends to change us into what we eat."[46] This is very different from taking normal food. Usually when we eat our food it becomes assimilated into our bodies for energy, and some of the waste finds its way to the sewer. But the Eucharistic food, which is the Bread of Life, acts in the opposite way. Instead of assimilating Christ into our system, we are assimilated into him. St Augustine recalls Jesus revealing to him, "I am the food of the full-grown; grow, and you will eat me; and you will not change me into yourself like the food of your flesh, but *you will be changed into me.*"[47] Normal food is not a living thing, and consequently is not the source of life as such. It simply sustains the life we have by being assimilated into our bodies. The Bread of Life does the opposite. This bread gives life to those who receive it, assimilates them and transforms them into itself. We are changed by Christ who comes to live within us, and the change conforms us to him. Jesus makes us like him in our feelings, our desires, our attitudes and our way of thinking. He puts into us "the mind that was in Christ Jesus". (Phil 2:5)

Something wonderful is happening when we receive Jesus in Holy Communion. He draws us into his heart. He gives us his life. Jesus says, "As the living Father sent me, and I live because of the Father, so whoever eats me *will live because of me*" (Jn 6:57). This means that Jesus is the very source of our life, and the very means by which we continue to have life. Unless we eat of him we human beings will die. We certainly live "because of him" in the sense that we rely totally upon him for everything. As he says, using the image of the vine and branches, "cut off from me you can do nothing". He is our everything in the sense that our life depends totally upon him; without him we are totally lost and bereft of salvation and any hope of sanctification.

But we also live "because of him" in another sense. Because he is our source of life he also becomes our *very reason for living*. He is our hope, the one who provides meaning for our lives, gives direction and purpose to our existence. It is for Christ that we get up in the morning no matter what the day has in store for us. It is for Christ that we make the tough decisions of discipleship without counting the cost. It is for Christ that we lay down our lives in service of others, loving until it hurts. We don't want any more to live our lives for ourselves only; we want to live our lives for Christ, and this means living our lives for others. We want to glory no longer in our own intelligence, or in our own achievements, or in our own adventures, but we want to glory only in the cross of Jesus, because through union with him we have discovered the fullness of life.

Witness from Prison

Because the Eucharist is so readily available to us we take it for granted. We become over familiar with it. Even though we subscribe to the doctrines, we fall into a routine in which we lose a sense of the magnificent treasure that has been given to us. Reading the stories of those who have been imprisoned and deprived of the Eucharist, can jolt us out of this spiritual lethargy and help us to realise that "we cannot live without the Lord's Supper".[48] In 1975, after Saigon had fallen to the Vietnamese communists, Bishop Francis Xavier Van Thuan had just been made coadjutor bishop of Saigon. He was arrested immediately and imprisoned for thirteen years. Nine of these were spent in solitary confinement.

When he was arrested a tormenting question dominated his thoughts, "Will I be able to celebrate Eucharist?" Stripped of everything else he hungered deeply for the Eucharist. The Eucharist is the food for the afflicted, the bread of hope. The day after he was arrested he was permitted to write to his people in order to ask for some necessities. He wrote, "Please send me a little wine as medicine for my stomach." They sent the bottle of wine with a label which read, "medicine for stomach aches". They also sent some hosts which they hid in a flashlight for protection against the humidity. He relates:

> I will never be able to express my great joy! Every day, with three drops of wine and a drop of water in the palm of my hand, I would celebrate Mass. This was my altar, and this was my cathedral! It was true medicine for soul and body...Each time I celebrated the Mass, I had the opportunity to extend my hands and nail myself to the cross with Jesus, to drink with him the bitter chalice. Each day in reciting the words of consecration, I confirmed with all my heart and soul a new pact, an eternal pact between Jesus and me through his blood mixed with mine. Those were the most beautiful Masses of my life![49]

10

THE BLOOD OF JESUS WASHES US CLEAN

> "He has entered the sanctuary once and for all, taking with him not the blood of goats and bull calves, but his own blood, having won an eternal redemption for us." (Heb 9:12)

The Price of our Redemption

From the opened side of Christ on the cross his blood flowed copiously. St Alphonsus Liguori says that one drop of his blood would have been sufficient to redeem us, but to demonstrate his excessive love, he shed the last drop of his blood for us. It speaks of the fullness of his mercy. We have been purchased by the blood of Jesus; that is we have been made God's own. Paul says, "You are not your own property. You have been bought and paid for with a price" (1 Cor 6:20). And the price paid for our redemption was not silver or gold, but the precious blood of Jesus (1 Pet 1:18-19). Like the Israelites of old who were protected from the avenging angel by the blood of the lamb that was daubed on their lintels, so we also have been delivered from the powers of darkness by the blood of the Lamb of God. The Lord told Catherine of Siena "not to think of your sins without calling to mind the blood and the greatness of my mercy".[50] Jesus is the one "who loves us and freed us from our sins by his blood". (Rev 1:5)

Let us look at a fundamental text on redemption, which is at the hub of Paul's message to the Romans. Paul says we are all "justified by his grace as a gift, through the redemption that is in Christ Jesus, whom God put forward as a sacrifice of atonement by his blood, effective through faith" (Rom 3:24-25). This term "atonement" is sometimes translated as "expiation". The Greek word is *"hilasterion"*, which is a translation of the Hebrew, *"kapporet"*, meaning "mercy seat". In the Old Testament the mercy seat was the golden cover on the Ark of the Covenant in the Holy of Holies. On the Day of Atonement, or *"Yom Kippur,"* the High Priest went into the Holy of Holies and sprinkled the "mercy seat" with blood of the bull which had been killed as a sin offering. This blood was understood to wash away the stain of the sins committed by the people in the previous year. Now Paul is proclaiming that Jesus is the one and final "mercy seat."

When Paul designates Jesus as the new definitive "mercy seat" he means that Jesus radically surpasses the effectiveness of the old one in bringing purification. In his self-offering on the cross Jesus brings all the sin of the world deep within the love of God, and wipes it away. In the old dispensation, the blood of animals by touching a holy object was seen as effecting reconciliation between God and humanity. However, the sacrifices of old were never sufficient to purify us of our sins. Now with Jesus, the new "mercy seat," we are cleansed totally by his blood and it does not need to be repeated again. As the sin of humanity, which is laid upon Jesus, is brought into contact with the infinite goodness and love in the heart of Christ, love conquers hatred, goodness conquers evil, forgiveness conquers violence.

The Blood of Jesus Purifies

We are now assured that there is power in the blood to sanctify us. As John says, "the blood of Jesus, his Son, purifies us from all sin" (1 Jn 1:7). And in Hebrews we read, "He has entered the sanctuary once and for all, taking with him *not* the blood of goats and bull calves, but *his own blood*, having won an eternal redemption for us." The old sacrifices could only purify from outward actions, but the blood of Jesus "can purify our inner self from dead actions so that we do our service to the living God" (Heb 9:14). In the light of this truth the Lord tells Catherine of Siena, "No one ought to despair. No, reach out trustingly for the blood, no matter what sins you have committed, for my mercy, which you receive in the blood, is incomparably greater than all the sins that have ever been committed in the world."[51]

We need to be convinced of the power in the blood of Jesus. We need to have faith in the blood, and come confidently to the sacrament which ministers to us the blood of the Redeemer, and receive the blood in Holy Communion. The blood can purify deep hidden areas of hardness of heart and sinful resistance within us to God's plan. We need to bathe in the blood of Jesus. Catherine is quite extravagant in her language:

> Drown yourself in the blood of Jesus crucified, bathe yourself in the blood, inebriate and satiate yourself with the blood and clothe yourself in the blood. And if you are unfaithful, baptise yourself again in the blood; if the devil has blurred your mind's eye, cleanse your eyes with the blood; if you become ungrateful for unseen gifts, be grateful in the blood ... Melt your lukewarmness in the heat of the blood and in the light of the blood darkness will dissolve and you will be the spouse of Truth.[52]

In case we find the language extreme, remember that the blood of Jesus is an instrument of his great mercy. We are to be cleansed and become inebriated by his mercy.

When we come to Holy Communion it is good to drink the blood of Jesus into those areas of the heart that are struggling the most. Maybe it is areas of sinfulness, sicknesses of the heart, or deeply ingrained habits of the heart, which seem to have roots too deep for us to wrench out ourselves. In all of us there are deep levels of primal disorder that need the grace and mercy of God to break their stronghold. We know that a large proportion of our interior life is submerged below consciousness and needs the healing, saving power of God. We can drink the blood of Jesus into our minds and hearts, soaking not only the conscious level, but the semi-conscious level and the unconscious as well. We need to acknowledge our interior poverty and utter incapacity to bring about our redemption and transformation. All we can do is call upon the saving mercy of God to penetrate the darkness and bring his wonderful light. By deliberately drinking the precious blood of Jesus into these troublesome areas we are eventually set free.

Forgiveness of Sins

Eucharist is a wonderful sacrament of forgiveness of sins. The blood we drink in the Eucharist was "shed for the many, for the forgiveness of sins". Being united to Christ in Holy Communion we are cleansed of past sins and preserved from future sins.[53] St Ambrose wrote:

> For as often as we eat this bread and drink this cup, we proclaim the death of the Lord. If we proclaim the Lord's death, we proclaim the forgiveness of sins. If, as often as his blood is poured out, it is poured for the forgiveness of sins, I should always receive it, so that it may always forgive my sins. Because I always sin, I should always have a remedy.[54]

Of course this reflection on the blood of Jesus is an exhortation to receive communion under both kinds as often as possible. It was clear at the Last Supper that Jesus offered the cup to all, not only to some. For practical reasons, and also as a result of some historical factors, communion under both kinds is not the normal way many today receive Holy Communion. We know, by the doctrine of "concomitance", that when we receive the consecrated host alone we receive the body, blood, soul and divinity of Jesus Christ. Yet, something is missing in the sign value of the sacrament when the chalice is not given. The sacrament expresses the Lord's passion, and certainly the shedding of his blood was essential to this reality. So it is most appropriate that the cup be shared, not for sake of validity, but for the participation of the faithful who seek the full benefit of the sacrament (not being satisfied with the precious blood due to concomitance alone). One helpful text from Rome states:

> Holy Communion more completely expresses its nature of sign when it is received under both kinds. The sign of the Eucharistic banquet is more evident and the divine will to sanction the new and everlasting covenant in the Lord's Blood is more clearly expressed, and the link between the Eucharistic banquet and the eschatological banquet of the Father's kingdom is clearer.[55]

11

COMMUNION IN THE BODY OF CHRIST

"All of us in union with Christ form one body, and as part of it we belong to each other." (Rom 12:5)

Community Celebrates

In our age marked by rampant individualism the full meaning of Eucharistic communion can elude us. We can be governed by a consumer mentality whereby we individually shop around for the "best" Eucharistic celebration so that our spiritual sensitivities can be satisfied. But this attitude leaves us desperately impoverished of genuine Eucharistic spirituality. If we confine our experience of Eucharist to our own private sphere and have no connection with communal reality we are missing the point. Our spirituality is seriously diminished if we treat the Mass like a service station, where we drive in, fill up the tank, and drive out totally disconnected from the community which celebrates. We do ourselves a disservice if we use the Eucharist in a similar way to a "fast food" outlet; just drive in, eat the favoured food, pay, and drive away satisfied. These images are possibly unfair and derogatory but unfortunately convey some truth. Eucharist is the celebration of a community of the faithful; it is not only a private devotional practice, no matter how piously we may pray to God. The Catholic Catechism reminds us, "It is the whole community, the body of Christ united with its Head, that celebrates."[56]

We must not forget our baptismal identity: "You are a chosen race, a royal priesthood, a consecrated nation, a people set apart to sing the praises of God who called you out of the darkness into his wonderful light. Once you were not a people at all and now you are the people of God; once you were outside the mercy and now you have been given mercy." (1 Pet 2:9-10)

Criterion of Authenticity

This profoundly communal dimension of the Eucharist is essential for its authenticity. The earliest witness to the Eucharist in the New Testament is found in St Paul's first letter to the Corinthians. The letter was written to correct a series of problems in the community that had been reported to Paul. Writing from Ephesus he rebuked them because of the divisions they had allowed to exist. There were a number of factions and the community was consequently fractured. Within this context Paul presents the Eucharistic table as a place of union. He summons the members of the community to remember the death of Jesus, the gift of himself on the cross for them. How can the community which was founded on the preaching of the *kerygma*, the proclamation of the saving death and resurrection of Jesus, and remembers that paschal mystery at Eucharist, be divided between the "strong" and the "weak", between the "haves" and the "have-nots"? Are the Corinthians willing to live the reality of the cross of Jesus in their lives? Their community is meant to proclaim the death of Jesus until he comes; and that is what their Eucharistic ritual proclaims also. But the ritual had become empty because the community was not living the way of Jesus authentically.

It is possibly surprising to us that Paul regarded the Eucharist celebrated in Corinth as seriously diminished and unfruitful, precisely because their *community life* was inauthentic and not true to the gospel. The essence of Paul's reaction was that there can be no authentic

Eucharist in a community if it is fractured into cliques or factions, or if it is divided on racial lines or other ethnic prejudices, or if there is disregard for the poor. To the extent that these problems exist the Eucharistic liturgy is rendered impoverished and celebrated unworthily. It cannot bear good fruit. Paul is emphasising that the foundation for an authentic celebration of Eucharist is that there be a community which is converted to Christ and working hard on unity through learning to join themselves with the sacrifice of Christ and hence to love one another. The Eucharist is firstly an expression of this communion of love in Christ, and secondly a means for this communal love to be deepened. This perspective has profound implications for the way we approach receiving Holy Communion.

Communion in the Body of Christ

While it is a beautiful and powerful means of personal transformation, the Eucharist is first and foremost a *communal reality*. The communion song and procession are meant to express that we are *moving together* towards the table of the Lord, from which we partake of the banquet, so we can become more one in him. The Eucharist deepens us in being Church. "The bread that we break, is it not a participation in the body of Christ? Because there is one bread, we who are many are one body, for we all partake of the one bread" (1 Cor 11:17-34). The word "body" is used twice in this text. The first time it designates the real body of Christ, given in the consecrated bread which we receive. The second time it refers to the "one body", which is the Church. This explains clearly that Eucharistic communion is both communion with God and communion with one another. The following words from Augustine are worth pondering:

> If you wish then to understand the body of Christ, listen to the Apostle as he says to the faithful, "You are the body of Christ and his members" (1 Cor 12:27). If, therefore, you are

the body of Christ and his members, your mystery has been placed on the Lord's table, and you receive your mystery. You reply "Amen" to that which you are ... Be a member of the body of Christ so that your "Amen" may be true.[57]

This means that on the altar after the consecration there are two bodies - the *real* body of Christ, born of the Virgin Mary, crucified and risen, and the *mystical* body of Christ. The body of Jesus, who is both Priest and Victim, is being offered for the salvation of the world. The body of the Church is being offered with him because we have freely responded to his love and placed ourselves as Church on the altar as a living sacrifice. This is the only authentic way we can participate in the Mass. Our offering, that of the Church and its members, is nothing without Christ. But with Christ it is a fragrant offering to God. Of course, Christ's offering lacks nothing in providing redemption for all men and women. In that sense he does not need our offering. Yet, so that his salvation may reach to the ends of the earth he needs our participation. In that sense we make up "what is lacking in the suffering of Christ".

This also means that when we receive Holy Communion we receive both the real body of Christ, which is the real presence of Christ given for us. But in receiving Christ we also receive ourselves as well, in the sense that we are confirmed more deeply in who we are as the body of Christ, and empowered to become more fully who we are. Thus the Eucharist builds the Church. This means that we not only celebrate the Eucharist, but that in and through Jesus, we must *become* Eucharist.

St Augustine encouraged us to believe that we "become the body of Christ by eating the body of Christ". He said "we are his body and through his mercy we are what we receive".[58] Speaking to adult converts he goes on to describe how bread is made from many grains of wheat which are ground together to make flour, and then baked in the oven. He says the new converts have been like that. The many grains have been ground by those who gave the good news to them, and by repentance and fasting as they prepared for baptism, and then they came to the waters of baptism, and were kneaded and became one. The fire of the Holy Spirit came on them and they were baked and became the bread of the Lord. He is saying that the body of Christ, the Church, is formed through the same pain and struggle that made the Eucharistic bread. The Eucharistic bread, once received, causes the unity that it signifies. What is visibly symbolised by the bread and wine (through the unity of many grains of wheat and the multiplicity of grapes) the sacrament brings about in our hearts, binding us together in the Spirit. This will only happen if we are committed to it; that is if we are intent upon being the faith-filled and loving community that God calls us to be.

Amen to the Body of Christ

The challenge for the Christian community is to be authentic in its proclamation of the death and resurrection of Jesus by the way its members love one another in him. If the community is racked with dissension, factions, unresolved conflict, bitterness, judgements and the like, then to that extent the Eucharistic celebration will not bring about the fruit it is meant to produce. And in fact those who celebrate Eucharist are living a lie and will be under God's judgement because of it. Paul makes this clear when he says:

> Until the Lord comes, therefore, every time you eat this bread and drink this cup, you are proclaiming his death, and so anyone who eats the bread or drinks the cup unworthily will be behaving unworthily towards the body and blood of the Lord. Everyone is to recollect himself before eating this bread and drinking this cup; because a person who eats and drinks without recognising the body is eating and drinking his own condemnation (1 Cor 11:26-29).

There are some who interpret the "the body" in this passage to mean the real presence of Jesus in the Eucharist. There are others who interpret it to mean the "body of Christ", the Church. Probably both interpretations are right. Not to recognise, or not to "discern", the body is to fail to recognise the real presence of the Lord as the one who died for us, giving himself over for us in love. He did this precisely so that we would be formed into the one body, the Church. So when we are about to receive Holy Communion the priest says "The body of Christ!" and we reply "Amen!" We say "Amen" firstly to the real presence of the sacred body of Jesus, born of the Virgin Mary, who died and rose again for us. But we also say "Amen" to his body, the Church, of which we are members. While they are distinct, we cannot separate the two bodies. We cannot have the one without the other. When we receive Communion we cannot be self-enclosed in a pious cocoon, shutting out the relationships with our brothers and sisters in Christ.

When we are not reconciled with another in the body, or when there is some unfortunate tension in the relationship we need to deal with this if we are going to be an authentic participant in the Eucharistic worship. But if things are as yet unresolved we need to remember that Pope Francis reminded us that the Eucharist is "not a prize for the perfect but a powerful medicine and nourishment for the weak".[59] In this case we approach the altar bringing the unresolved situation with us, and especially bringing with us the person or persons involved. We can acknowledge our weakness to the Lord. Every Communion brings us more intimately into the experience of Jesus crucified. We can stand together with the one from whom we are estranged at the foot of the cross and beg the mercy that we need to attain the unity of which this Communion speaks. We show our readiness to die with Jesus. The one thing we cannot do is to ignore the other members of the body with apathy or indifference, or dismiss them as of no importance, since that attitude would be to eat and drink to our condemnation.

Genuine Communion of Hearts

In the dominant culture today we glorify the strong, the handsome and the successful. We tend to overlook, or even reject the weak and vulnerable. In this regard a genuine Eucharistic community will be counter cultural. There is a thirst in the heart of every person for friendship and communion of hearts, which goes even beyond being a generous giver. I can generously bestow gifts on others with kindness, but still remain in control; it is more condescension than mutual love. It lacks vulnerability. Rather than be a community where people think only about themselves and their own success, Eucharist builds a culture of acceptance and hospitality for all, especially the weak and marginalised.

Jean Vanier, founder of L'Arche, tells the story of a young boy who had a serious handicap, and was making his first Holy Communion in a church in Paris.[60] After the Eucharist there was a family gathering. The uncle, who was also the child's godfather, told the mother: "What a beautiful liturgy, how sad that he didn't understand a thing". The boy heard these words and his eyes filled with tears. He said to his mother: "Don't worry Mum, Jesus loves me just as I am." The child had a wisdom that the uncle had not yet attained. This boy knew the wonderful gift of Eucharist; that Jesus loves him, no matter what physical or mental capacities he lacked.

In the cry for communion of hearts which we hear in the weak and vulnerable, the cry for welcome and acceptance, there is a cry for communion with Jesus in the Eucharist. We need to get in touch with that cry within our own hearts. It is a cry for relationship and communion of hearts which makes us more open to God, who is all about relationship and love. Jesus came to draw us into communion with him and through him with the Father, so that we will have deeper communion with one another. The disciples were expecting him to be generous and perform many miracles for them and for others, but they were taken aback when they realised that what Jesus wanted most was communion with them. We are to make ourselves vulnerable to Jesus coming to us, and in that communion of hearts we become more vulnerable to one another. We relinquish our hold on superior competence or status or knowledge or power, and join with others in a oneness of heart without distinctions made by prejudice and social proprieties. We discover communion with one another in Jesus.

In Eucharist we are already celebrating the heavenly banquet. A parable may help. A holy man was given a vision of hell. He saw a large banquet hall with a table laden with delicious food of every kind. The people at the table were full of anger and frustration. The only way they could eat the food was with elongated knives and forks and spoons which were so long that it was impossible to get the food to their mouths. They lived in the eternal agony of having the prize before them but being deprived of it. Then the holy man was given a vision of heaven. To his surprise there was a similar large table with a vast array of extravagant dishes. And the people had to use same utensils for eating. To his delight the man saw that in this case everyone was full of eternal joy. What was the difference? Instead of each one trying to feed himself or herself, in the heavenly banquet they were using the implements to feed one another.

12

THE WASHING OF THE FEET

"For I have set you an example, that you also should do as I have done." (Jn 13:15)

He Loved them to the End

In John's gospel there is no institution narrative. The reason is that John's emphasis is on the event of the new Passover, which, as we have seen, he identifies clearly as the Lamb of God being slain on the cross for our sake. He presumes the liturgical celebration of the new Passover, which would have been well in place by the time he wrote his gospel. All the same he has a profound presentation of the Last Supper, which focuses upon Jesus washing the feet of his disciples. There is no doubt that for John the washing of the feet expresses what is most significant about the Eucharist. He places this account at the very hinge of the gospel's classic diptych structure between "The Book of Signs" and "The Book of Glory". It carries one of the most significant themes of the evangelist – Christian love as the call to humble service.

We are told by John, that just before the Passover, "Jesus knew that his hour had come to depart from this world and go to the Father" (Jn 13:1). This "hour" had been predicted throughout the gospel, the "hour" of his glorification. Now it has come; now is to be revealed the fullness of the love of the Father for the world, and the immensity of love in the heart of the Son, who is to be offered as the sacrificial lamb for the world, and through his liberating death and resurrection to "pass over" to the Father. We are told, "Having loved his own in the world he loved them to the end." Now Jesus was going to show how perfect his love was; how complete and unconditional is his surrender to the Father's love and his self-giving love for us. Out of this excessive love in the heart of Jesus the Eucharistic life of the Church is formed.

Do as I have done

The Supper is eaten together in an atmosphere of warmth, affection and intense love. But also there is a dark brooding presence of the murderous designs of the ruler of this world. "The devil had already put it into the heart of Judas son of Simon Iscariot to betray him" (Jn 13:2). Jesus is totally given to the goodness of the Father's love, wanting to give us the example that we most need to be able to genuinely celebrate Eucharist into the future. He wanted to show us how we are to live if we are to be in union with him. He wanted to demonstrate that if we want to be with and for him, it means to be with and for one another. He got up from table and "took off his outer robe". This was a sign of not standing on ceremony, nor clinging to any worldly status. He then "tied a towel around himself". He was about to perform a menial task usually reserved for a household servant or slave.

As he is washing the feet of his disciples he comes to Peter who protests, "You shall never wash my feet!" Jesus responds by letting Peter know that what he is doing implies something essential in their relationship, "Unless I wash you, you will have no share with me." Peter responds extravagantly, "Then, Lord, not only my feet but my hands and my head as well." Jesus then explains to them what this sign means. Communion with him means imitating his self-giving love. "If

I then, the Lord and Master, have washed your feet, you should wash each other's feet" (Jn 13:14-15). We are to do as he has done.

Who is the greatest?

Interestingly in Luke's gospel during the Last Supper a dispute arose amongst the disciples as to who was the greatest. Jesus resolved it by reminding them that it is the pagans who lord it over one another. But they are not to be like this. "Who is the greater; the one at table or the one who serves? The one at table surely? Yet here am I among you as one who serves!" (Lk 22:27) Was it this dispute that sparked off Jesus' washing of the feet? We do not know. But we do know that this theme is central to all the gospels. In Mark's gospel the disciples were arguing along the way about who was the greatest, and Jesus called them to him and said, "If anyone wants to be first, he must make himself last of all and servant of all" (Mk 9:15). And somewhat later when James and John had caused a stir by claiming the seats at the right hand and the left of the kingdom, Jesus told them, "You know that among the pagans their so-called rulers lord it over them, and their great men make their authority felt. This is not to happen among you. No; anyone who wants to become great among you must be your servant, and anyone who wants to be first among you must be slave to all. For the Son of Man himself did not come to be served but to serve, and to give his life *as a ransom for the many*." (Mk 10:42-45)

The "washing of the feet" is an action by Jesus which shows us that our lives are to be for others, not for ourselves. His going to the Cross in self-giving love is to win us and persuade us into a new way of being with one another. By participating in the Eucharistic sacrifice we are called out of our self-seeking attitudes. We are to act as Christ acted. Our lives are not to be about what we get from others, but rather what we can give. This is a love that "does not insist on its own interests" (*cf.* 1 Cor 13:5). If we have a true spirit of service we will not be intent on pleasing ourselves, but in caring for the needs of others. We will not be feathering our own nest for the sake of our own comfort, guarding our free time, making an idol of our rest. The rule will be always be according to the way of the Master: "Christ did not please himself." (Rom 15:3)

Emptied Himself

This theme of service is at the heart of the redemptive work of Jesus. We are reminded of the hymn in Philippians: "Let the same mind be in you that was in Christ Jesus." We are to imitate Jesus: "Though he was in the form of God he did not cling to his equality with God, but he *emptied himself* taking the form of a servant (a slave)" (Phil 2:6-7). This self-emptying of Jesus was expressed in his becoming like us in all things but sin, but then he humbled himself even further by being obedient unto death on the cross. This is the only authentic way of imitating Jesus. The whole of Jesus' life from beginning to the end was a washing of the feet, a profound act of self-giving love, of humility and obedience unto death. Every time we celebrate Eucharist we are invited more deeply into this dynamic, and we are given the power to love unto the end, to humble ourselves before others, and to serve until it hurts.

The humility of Jesus did not mean that he renounced his rightful authority as Lord and Master, but that he lowered himself before others in self-forgetful service. True humility is not found in self-denigrating attitudes, but in the practical behaviour of love that seeks the interests of others first and seeks to serve their needs. Jesus is our model. In the Eucharist we are able to draw from him the power of love that is in his heart to be able to love as he has loved. St Francis of Assisi exclaimed, "Look at God's humility, my brothers, and pour out your hearts before him. Humble yourselves so that you may be exalted by him. Keep nothing for yourselves, so that he who has given himself wholly to you may receive you wholly."[61]

We notice that Jesus did not say to his disciples that he did not want them to aspire towards greatness. Rather, he said, "if anyone wants to be great among you he must become your servant". We should desire greatness, but not the "greatness" of the celebrities of this world, seeking money, power, and status. Rather we want to be great in God, through imitating him in his humility. This does not mean belittling ourselves in the eyes of others, or having a low opinion of ourselves. God *is not* little. He is all powerful, and his greatness has no measure because his love endures forever. Nor does God *feel* little. That would be impossible. However God *made himself little* by becoming one of us, and emptying himself further by dying on the cross as a common criminal. By washing the feet of his disciples Jesus makes himself little before them. This is what Paul means when he urges us to always treat the other as "better" than ourselves (Phil 2:3). Others are my "better", not because of any mistaken sense of inferiority before them; but because I choose to give them the honour, respect and service, which is like that given by slaves in ancient times to their masters (their "betters"). This call to service is the trade-mark of humility. In Eucharist we are formed in this virtue.

PART IV

PRESENCE

O Sacrum Convivium

O sacrum convivium!	O sacred Banquet!
in quo Christus sumitur:	in which Christ is received,
recolitur memoria passionis eius:	the memory of his Passion is renewed,
mens impletur gratia:	the mind is filled with grace,
et futurae gloriae nobis pignus datur. Alleluia.	and a pledge of future glory to us is given. Alleluia.

Thomas Aquinas

Ave Verum Corpus

Ave verum corpus natum	Hail, true body born
de Maria Virgine,	of the Virgin Mary, who
vere passum, immolatum	having truly suffered, was sacrificed
in cruce pro homine	on the cross for mankind,
cuius latus perforatum	whose pierced side
fluxit aqua et sanguine:	flowed with water and blood:
esto nobis praegustatum	may it be for us a foretaste
in mortis examine.	in the trial of death
O Iesu dulcis, O Iesu pie,	O sweet Jesus, O merciful Jesus
O Iesu, fili Mariae	O Jesus, son of Mary,
miserere mei. Amen	have mercy on me. Amen

13

THE REAL PRESENCE

"Whoever eats of this bread will live forever; and the bread that I will give is my flesh for the life of the world." (Jn 6:51)

Four Presences

Christ is really present in many ways in the life of the Church. In the Church's Eucharistic liturgy he is present firstly in the people gathered. Jesus promised, "where two or three are gathered in my name I am in the midst" (Mt 18:20). This is the most fundamental of the liturgical presences of Christ. The other modes of his presence are all geared towards deepening this ecclesial communion in him. Christ is also really present in the word when it is proclaimed in the assembly. In a particular way, when the gospel is proclaimed Christ speaks to his people. This aims to bring the people gathered to a deeper conversion as disciples and leads them into a deeper communion with him. He is also present in the priest who is acting in the liturgy "in persona Christi Capitis" i.e. in the person of Christ as Head of the body. When the priest preaches, prays the Eucharistic prayer, and pronounces the words of institution it is Christ who is present. The priest is acting in the name of Christ, and it is Christ who acts in and through the priest. However, the most "dense" presence of Christ is under the appearance of bread and wine after the consecration. Pope Paul VI explained: "This presence is called 'real' – by which is not intended to exclude the other types of presence as if they could not be 'real' too, but because it is presence in the fullest sense; that is to say, it is a *substantial* presence by which Christ, God and man, makes himself wholly and entirely present."[62] It is an entirely *unique* mode of presence. Even the word "real" could leave us impoverished in understanding, since the word is derived from the Latin *res*, which means a thing or an object. But Jesus is not present in the Eucharist as a "thing" or an object, but rather as a person.

Biblical Faith

The biblical faith in the real presence of Jesus in the Eucharist is compelling. The best testimony is in chapter 6 of John's gospel. After a dialogue in which Jesus identifies himself as the "bread of life" for which all people hunger, and "the bread come down from heaven", his interlocutors begin to complain. But he does not back off in any way. Rather he presses further, "Anyone who eats this bread will live forever; and the bread that I shall give is my flesh, for the life of the world" (Jn 6:51). At this point "the Jews" begin arguing amongst themselves. How can this man give them his flesh? The idea was repulsive. It was a strong prohibition of the Law not to partake of flesh or blood of any kind (Gen 9:3-4; Lev 3:17; Deut 12:23). If it was nauseating for the Jews to eat of the flesh and drink the blood of animals, how much more repulsive it would have been to suggest eating the flesh and blood of a human being! But Jesus did not in any way soften the teaching or suggest he was simply using symbolic language. Rather he pushes forward using even more realistic terms, "Very truly, I tell you, unless you eat the flesh of the Son of Man and drink his blood, you have no life in you" (Jn 6:53). The Greek word used for "eat" here is *trogein* which was usually employed to describe how animals munch their food. Jesus could have used the word *phagein* which one would expect for ordinary eating. But he uses the stronger word to emphasise that he really means for us to actually eat him. He goes on to say "my flesh is real food and my blood is real drink". Nothing could be clearer.

Why does Jesus give himself to us in this way? At the Last Supper he said "Take and eat", "Take and drink". He is not giving us his body and blood simply as a miracle of presence for us to adore; not simply to look at as object of veneration. No. His love for us is so great that he seeks intimate union with us, and if we consume his flesh and blood, his presence within us will in turn transform us. Jesus says, "As the living Father sent me, and I live because of the Father, so the one whoever eats me will live because of me" (Jn 6:57). This means that Jesus is the very source of our life, and the very means by which we continue to have life. Unless we eat of him we human beings will die. This is an extraordinary reality. The Greek word *trogein* emphasises this. The word was often used to refer to animals eating their staple diet. So horses eat hay, and cats go for milk, and monkeys for bananas. The implication is that the staple diet for human beings is the flesh of Christ! This is the food which keeps us going; the food by which we live. This is our "daily bread". We live due to the life Christ gives us or we do not live at all. Jesus gives himself to us because this is the way we will have fullness of life. He is not just a wise teacher or a good example to follow. He gives himself to us so that if we abide in him and he abides in us we can have the power to live his teaching and follow his example as his disciples.

When Jesus offers us his flesh to eat, and his blood to drink, we need to understand what is meant biblically by "flesh" and "blood". By offering his flesh to us he is speaking of his whole human being in bodily form. By offering his blood to us he is speaking of his whole human being from the point of view of his interiority. His language was so realistic that his listeners misunderstood him, since they thought he was asking them to be cannibals. Many of those who had followed him to this point said, "This is intolerable language. How could anyone accept it?" His answer to this was not to in any way to ameliorate the language but rather to ask another question, "Does this upset you? What if you should see the Son of Man ascend to where he was before?" In other words he was not speaking of his physical body in the mode they were now seeing him, but rather of his glorified risen body. Because of the resurrection he can give himself to us really as his flesh and blood, but in a sacramental manner. We partake of the one Christ, Jesus of Nazareth, born of the Virgin Mary, crucified and now glorified. Because Christ is now glorified, this unique mode of Eucharistic presence is possible.

Faith of the Fathers

In the early Church the teaching of the real presence was affirmed, but it was not the central focus of attention. It was simply presumed on the basis of the strong New Testament witness. Around 150 AD Justin Martyr, writing to the pagan Emperor, outlined the Christian belief, "We call this food by the name of the Eucharist. It is not permitted to eat of it if one does not believe it to be what we teach ... namely Jesus Christ who by means of the word of God ... changes this into his body and blood."[63] In the catechetical talks given by Cyril of Jerusalem, when discussing the Eucharist, he reads to his listeners St Paul's account of the words of institution at the Last Supper. Then he comments, "This teaching of St Paul is designed to give you certitude regarding these mysteries through which you become one in body and one in blood with Christ." And then he adds, "If he has thus affirmed that this is my blood, who then could entertain any doubts or say that this is not his blood?"[64] St Ambrose of Milan in the fourth century underlined the consistent faith of the Church when he insisted of the Eucharist: "Prior to being consecrated, it is bread, but when the words of Christ have been added to it, it is the body of Christ."[65] St John Chrysostom in the fourth century also articulates emphatically the power that brings the change to the bread and wine: "It is not a human being who can change the offerings of the body and blood of Christ, but Christ himself, crucified for us ... The priest pronounces certain words, but the power and the grace of God are present."[66] These fathers of the Church stress the power of God at work in the consecration. Obviously they are not speaking of simply a symbolic presence, but rather a real presence that cannot be produced by the priest or any other human being, but can only come about by the power of God. St Augustine adds his voice to this line of patristic witnesses. He says, "That which you see, beloved, on the altar of the Lord is bread and wine, but this bread and wine, once the word has come over them, become the body and blood of the Word ... In fact, take away this word and there is only bread and wine; add this word and there is something else. And what is this something else? The body and blood of Christ."[67]

It is not only the word spoken by Christ through the priest at the consecration which brings about the conversion of the bread and wine into the body and blood of Christ. The change also happens through the power of the Holy Spirit. The Eastern fathers emphasise this dimension, regarding the *epiclesis*, or invocation, of the Holy Spirit before the consecration as the moment of change, and the word of the priest as a confirmation of this. Theodore of Mopsuestia wrote:

> By virtue of the liturgical action, it is as if Our Lord were risen from the dead and pours his grace on all of us, through the Holy Spirit ... When the priest declares that the bread and wine are the Body and Blood of Christ, he affirms that this has come about through the Holy Spirit. It is the same as what happened to Christ's natural body when it received the Holy Spirit and his unction. At the moment the Holy Spirit comes, we believe they are the body and blood of Christ, immortal, incorruptible, impassible and immutable by nature, like the body of Christ at resurrection.[68]

We don't have to put these two "moments" in competition with one another, either the moment of epiclesis or the moment of the words of consecration. This is a good example of how the East and West are as "two lungs" of the one Church of Christ. It is not a case of choosing "either or" but rather "both and". The Catholic Catechism combines the two perspectives by stating, "The Church fathers strongly affirmed the faith of the Church in the efficacy of the word of Christ and of the action of the Holy Spirit to bring about this conversion."[69] The Eastern focus on the action of the Holy Spirit brings a new richness to our understanding of the Eucharist, and since Vatican Council II the invocation of the Holy Spirit in the Eucharistic prayers have been highlighted. Eucharistic prayer III, after acknowledging that God gives life to all things and makes them holy by the power of the Holy Spirit moves into the *epiclesis* as the priest extends his hands over the bread and wine, "Therefore, O Lord, we humbly implore you: by the same Spirit graciously make holy these gifts we have brought to you for consecration, that they may become the body and blood of your Son our Lord Jesus Christ."

Challenge to the faith

Focus on the theology of the real presence became more intense in the eleventh century when a monk, Berengarius of Tours, proposed that, at the consecration, the bread and wine were not essentially changed, but were infused with spiritual power as a result of becoming a "sign of a sacred reality". He claimed to be simply developing the teaching of St Augustine, but had misunderstood the latter's teaching. He argued that the consecrated bread and wine is not actually the glorified body of Jesus, but a sign pointing towards it. His teaching caused an immediate furore and met furious opposition. The voice that was most vociferous in opposition was that of Lanfranc of Bec, a Benedictine abbot, who called upon the witness of John 6, and also the teaching of the fathers. Berengarius' approach, he rightly argued, did not give sufficient due to the reality of the change that took place at the consecration. Pope Nicholas called a Synod in 1059 to resolve the debate. Berengarius was condemned and he was forced to recant and to make an oath that "the bread and wine which are placed on the altar are, after the consecration ... the true body and blood of our Lord Jesus Christ."[70]

In reaction to Berengarius, who did not give enough credence to the reality of the change, the pendulum swung towards what we might call a "gross realism". In fact the oath that Berengarius was forced to take contained something of this aberration. He had to say that the true body and blood of Christ was "handled and broken by the hands of the priest, torn by the teeth of the faithful".[71] Intending to combat the subjectivist approach of Berengarius his opponents provided this formula which betrayed a gross physicality, coming close to the mentality of the Jews in John's gospel who thought Jesus was asking them to be cannibals. This crude realism did not eventually prevail, since it is not the true meaning of Jesus in John 6. St Augustine had maintained clearly that the presence of Jesus in the Eucharist is not his physical body as it was prior to the resurrection, but that of his glorious, risen body, present "in the sacrament". It is a sacramental not a physical presence, mediated by signs, and precisely by bread and wine. However, in this case the sign does not exclude the reality but makes the reality present to and for us. This is the only way that the body of the risen Christ can be substantially present to us while we are still on this earthly pilgrimage. Berengarius had misunderstood Augustine's understanding of sacrament. He thought Augustine was speaking only about a sign pointing to a sacred reality. But Augustine understood that in doing so the sacred reality was definitively made present.

Response to the Challenge

The next chapter in this fascinating history of the Church's faith in the real presence focuses around *how* the change takes place at the consecration. Here St Thomas Aquinas was the great champion. Drawing upon the philosophy of Aristotle that had been used by the Fourth Lateran Council, Thomas taught that at the consecration a change in substance occurred in the bread and wine while the appearances remain. The substances of the bread and wine change into the substances of the body and blood of Christ. The change takes place at the level beyond the senses; at the level of substance, that invisible substrate that makes up what a thing really is. Before the consecration if you ask, "What is this?" the answer is, "bread and wine". After the consecration if you ask, "What is this?" the answer is, "the body and blood of Christ". But the "accidents" or the "appearances" remain. If you see it, touch it, taste it, smell it, you can only detect what appears to be bread and wine. But the reality has changed. Thomas expresses it is his famous song *Adoro te devote*:

> Seeing, touching, tasting are in thee deceived; How says trusting hearing? That shall be believed; What God's Son has told me, take for truth I do; Truth himself speaks truly or there's nothing true.[72]

The senses deceive us. Even if, by a sacrilegious act, someone was to do a scientific experiment on the consecrated bread and wine, all they would find is what makes up bread and wine. The change takes place at a level beyond empirical scientific investigation. While the objective reality of the change is not at all dependent on our faith, it is only by faith in the word of God that we know it to be true. The Council of Trent, when combating the Reformers, who tended to favour an explanation akin to that of Berengarius, stated definitively:

> By the consecration of the bread and wine there takes place a change of the whole substance of the bread into the substance of the body of Christ our Lord and of the whole substance of the wine into the substance of his blood. This change the holy Catholic Church has fittingly and properly called transubstantiation.[73]

To leave us in no doubt of what the constant faith of the Church has been the Council then proclaimed that in the Eucharist "the body and blood, together with the soul and divinity, of our Lord Jesus Christ and , therefore, the whole Christ is truly, really, and substantially contained".[74]

We need to take notice of the three adverbs used by the Council: *vere, realiter, substantialiter*. Jesus is *truly* present and not just by sign or image or form. He is *really* present, and not only through the subjective faith of the believers. He is *substantially* present, that is, in a profound reality that cannot be seen by the senses. He is not present in the appearances, which remain that of bread and wine. In relation to this substantial presence it is important to notice that in ordinary life everything is not always as it appears. Sitting in a motionless train we can feel we are moving when we see another train moving on the track next to ours. Meeting a person we can quickly judge according to appearances and later find out they are not really like that at all. When we look at the consecrated bread and wine appearances deceive us. The reality has changed at a level beyond our sense perception. Our faith in the word of God tells us the truth.

Doubt no longer, but Believe

When the risen Jesus first appeared to his apostles in the upper room they were astounded and filled with joy. But Thomas, the apostle, was not with them. When they told him the good news he refused to believe. He wanted to see the evidence with his own eyes, and be able to touch Christ before he would believe, "Unless I see the holes that the nails made in his hands and can put my finger into the holes they made, and unless I can put my hand into his side, I refuse to believe" (Jn 20:19-29). There is possibly something of Thomas in all of us, especially in this scientific era when empirical evidence is demanded before anything can be truly believed. Many deny the existence of anything that cannot be verified by scientific experimentation. The doubting Thomas is well and truly alive today.

But returning to the story, when Jesus appeared again eight days later Thomas was in their midst. Jesus does not reproach Thomas but is sympathetic with his dilemma, "Put your finger here; look, here are my hands. Give me your hand; put it into my side. Doubt no longer but believe." We do not know whether Thomas actually did put his fingers on the wounds of Jesus. If he did, undoubtedly he would have experienced an "electric shock" of faith. But it seems that the point here is that he no longer needed to do so, but simply fell to his knees with the perfect act of adoration, "My Lord and my God!" Thomas is overwhelmed by the presence of the risen Christ. The only fitting response is total surrender and recognition of Jesus as Lord. The real point of the story now comes from the lips of Jesus, speaking to Thomas, "You believe because you can see me. Happy are those who have not seen and yet believe." This is the Eucharistic faith. How blessed we are that we do not see him, nor can we touch him, in the way that Thomas could. Yet we believe! We don't demand physical evidence. We aren't relying upon empirical investigation. We know the limits of our sensory perception, and of scientific investigation. But we know we have met the Lord; we know that when the Blessed Sacrament is exposed before us that we can only fall in reverence and awe before him in silent adoration because " something greater than Solomon is here". He is the Lord God, given for us.

A story is told of the other Thomas, Thomas Aquinas, the great theologian of mediaeval times. As we have seen how he brilliantly expounded the mystery of the Eucharist, and indeed the whole of the Catholic doctrine, using newly found Aristotelian philosophy. We still rely upon his thinking today. But his work was unfinished. Towards the end of his life as he was praying before the Blessed Sacrament, he had a moment of mystical revelation of the risen Christ present before him. He did not write again. His secretary asked him why he had stopped writing. Thomas replied, "All that I have written seems to be like so much straw compared to what I have seen and what has been revealed to me." He had been taken more deeply into the mystery of "the love of Christ which surpasses all knowledge". (Eph 3:19)

From Atheist to Love of God

In 1935 twenty-year-old Andre Frossard was working as a journalist in Paris. He was destined to become a leading writer of his time, and to be elected to *Academie Francaise*. His father had been one of the historic founders of the French Communist Party. Andre had been raised as an atheist, and considered religious practice as idiotic. Yet as a young man he had a friend who was a committed Catholic, who had tried unsuccessfully to lead him to belief in God. One evening the two friends were driving to the Latin Quarter to have dinner together. Andre's friend stopped the car outside a chapel where the Blessed Sacrament was perpetually exposed. He asked Andre to wait for him while he made a quick visit. After waiting a while Andre became impatient and getting out of the car entered the chapel. Standing at the back he looked around at the people praying, but could not find his friend. Looking toward the altar he turned his attention to the Blessed Sacrament exposed in the monstrance, but he had no idea what it was. Suddenly, to his great surprise he felt a mysterious power penetrate his heart. Later he recalled what he experienced at that moment:

> Having entered as a skeptic and an atheist ... indifferent and preoccupied with so many things other than God to whom I never even gave a thought even to deny ... I was standing by the door, looking around with my eyes for my friend, but did not succeed in finding him ... My gaze passed from the shadows to the light ... from the faithful gathered there, to the nuns, to the altar ... and came to rest above the second candle burning to the left of the Cross (unaware that I was gazing

on the exposed Blessed Sacrament). And at that point, suddenly a series of miracles unfolded whose indescribable force shattered in an instant the absurd being that I was, to bring to amazing birth the child that I had never been ... At first the hint of the words "spiritual life" came to me ... as if they had been pronounced in a whisper next to me ... then came a great light ... the brilliance of a world, another world of radiance and destiny such as to reduce ours to the faint shadows of unfinished dreams ... a world of sweetness and gentleness which was active and upsetting beyond every form of violence, capable of breaking the hardest stone and, harder than stone, the human heart. Its overflowing eruption, so complete, was accompanied by a joy which is the exultation of the saved, the joy of the shipwrecked who are rescued just in time. These sensations which I find difficult to adequately describe were all simultaneous ... Everything was dominated by the Presence ... of the One whose name I can never write again without feeling the dread of wounding his tenderness, the One before whom I have the happiness of being a forgiven child, woken up to learn that everything is gift.[75]

When Andre sought the priest for instruction in the faith he said "Nothing that the priest told me of Christian doctrine came as a surprise and I received it with joy." So much had been infused into him in that moment of encounter with Christ in the Blessed Sacrament. But he added, "One thing did surprise me, the Eucharist, not because it seemed to be unbelievable, but that divine love should have found this astounding way to communicate itself filled me with wonder, and most of all that bread was chosen, the staple of the poor and the favourite food of children. Of all the gifts heaped up before me by Christianity, this one was the most beautiful."

14

EUCHARISTIC ADORATION

"So you could not stay awake with me one hour?"
(Mt 26:40)

A Short History

The adoration of the Eucharist outside of the Mass is a relatively "new" innovation in the spiritual tradition of the Church. It first came to prominence in the eleventh century, partly in reaction to the Berengarius controversy. In the earlier centuries the Blessed Sacrament had been reserved for the sick and dying, at first in the sacristy of the church and then later in a niche in the wall of the sanctuary. However, in the Middle Ages when the focus of devotion came more upon the miraculous change of the bread and wine into the body and blood of Jesus, the faithful became more attentive to the awesome moment of consecration. The host was elevated for all to adore and express their faith in the real presence of Jesus. People rarely received Holy Communion due to an exaggerated sense of unworthiness. Eucharistic worship was primarily focused on the consecrated host which was to be adored rather than to be received. The age old popular practice of visiting churches to venerate the relics of saints hidden in the altar of sacrifice now shifted towards reverencing Jesus present in the reserved sacrament. The tabernacle now became more central and adorned. In Liege in Belgium, out of reaction to the Cathari heresy, which denied the reality of the incarnation, there arose a great wave of Eucharistic devotion which spread throughout Europe, and in 1264 this led to the institution of the feast of Corpus Christi by Pope Urban V.

All of this was a wonderful spiritual discovery for the Church. However, with the advent of Eucharistic processions, exposition of the Blessed Sacrament in elaborately adorned monstrances, and regular benediction, devotion to the Eucharist outside of Mass became more popular than the Mass itself. While attendance at Sunday Mass was imperative, reception of Holy Communion was sporadic. Daily Mass was mainly for priests and religious, and adoration of the Eucharist outside of Mass became the major focus of popular devotion. This imbalance began to be addressed at the beginning of the twentieth century when Pope Pius X strongly endorsed and encouraged all the faithful to come to daily Mass and receive Holy Communion. And then the liturgical renewal, generated in the universal Church before and after Vatican II, emphasised the centrality of the Eucharistic celebration itself. Adoration of the Blessed Sacrament outside of Mass was rightly seen to be secondary to the Mass.

Both Celebration and Contemplation

Unfortunately with the rediscovery of the centrality of the Eucharistic action, some began to dismiss Eucharistic adoration outside of Mass as an aberration. However, the Council had never intended to abolish adoration of the Blessed Sacrament, nor did it intend to demean it in the minds of the faithful. Eucharistic adoration is one of the special treasures that the Holy Spirit has provided. Every saint, since the time that this devotion became prevalent in the Church, has found it to be a wonderful source of sanctification. For example, St Alphonsus Liguori, who was combating the strict Jansenistic spirituality of his time, as well as his own personal battle with scruples, wrote, "of all devotions, that of adoring Jesus in the Blessed Sacrament is the greatest after the sacraments, the one dearest to God and the one most helpful to us".[76] Pope John Paul II testifies:

> It is pleasant to spend time with him, to lie close to his breast like the beloved disciple (*cf.* Jn 13:25) and to feel the infinite love present in his heart. If in our time Christians must be distinguished above all by the 'art of prayer', how can we not feel a renewed need to spend time in spiritual converse, in silent adoration, in heartfelt love before Christ present in the Most Holy Sacrament? How often, dear brothers and sisters, have I experienced this, and drawn from it strength, consolation and support![77]

In 1973 the Congregation for Divine Worship set out some principles. The adoration and worship of the Eucharist outside of the Mass is derived from the Eucharistic action and is directed towards it. The celebration of the Mass is what originates the devotion, and when we adore Jesus in the Blessed Sacrament we need to be hungering to receive him again in Holy Communion in the next Mass. The instruction insists (80) that "when the faithful worship Christ in the Blessed Sacrament they should recollect that this presence is derived from the sacrifice and evokes sacramental and spiritual communion".[78] Those who pray before Christ in the Blessed Sacrament "prolong that union which they have achieved with him in Holy Communion"[79] and they renew their commitment to live in the likeness of Christ in their daily lives.

When we pray before the Blessed Sacrament we are drawing upon all the graces of the Eucharist, receiving the power that flows from the death and resurrection of the Lord. Because it is an extension of the Eucharistic mystery which we have already celebrated and also leads us back to the celebration of this mystery, Eucharistic adoration makes available to us in faith the fruits of Christ's sacrifice. There are not two Eucharistic spiritualities, one for the celebration itself and the other for contemplation and adoration. There is only one

Eucharistic spirituality which embraces our whole life. Celebration and contemplation of the Eucharist do not exclude one another. Rather they complement one another beautifully.

The Wonder of Adoration

Contemplation of the Eucharist is an extraordinary privilege. Eucharistic devotion is founded in the mystery of the incarnation. St Irenaeus told us: "Mary first conceived the Word in her heart, and then in her womb." It would have been useless for her to carry Christ first in her womb and not to have carried him with love in her heart. We too must receive Christ into our hearts through contemplation before we receive his body. And we also dwell with him in heart to heart conversation after we have received his body. We gaze upon him in love as we behold him in the exposed Eucharist. St John Vianney observed one of his peasant parishioners spending long hours before Jesus in the Blessed Sacrament, and asked this fellow what he was doing during this time. The answer was simple, "He looks at me, and I look at him." This is contemplation. We need silence, a focus upon the Lord without undue distractions, a listening heart, and a desire for encounter. In our tiredness due to the busyness of life we may even drop off to sleep. All is not lost. After all the apostles did the same, which provoked the Lord to ask, "Can you not watch one hour with me?" But he knew their weakness. The most important thing is that you are there, and you want the Lord.

To spend time with the Beloved is to become like the Beloved. A change takes place in us imperceptibly as we spend time in adoration of Jesus in the Blessed Sacrament. Some have likened it to sunbathing. We cannot spend a long time exposed to the sun without it effecting a change on our faces. Similarly bathing in the sunshine of the love of Christ, letting his face shine upon us, we find change happens imperceptibly. Remaining in loving gaze upon our Beloved we begin to assimilate his thoughts, feelings and attitudes, not through reflectively thinking about it but in an intuitive way. Others have likened this dynamic to the process of photosynthesis in plants. Solar light works on the green leaves of plants, changing elements that they have absorbed from the atmosphere, giving much needed energy and nourishment to the plants. We open our hearts before Jesus, who like the sun radiates the light of love upon us. Like the green leaves, we draw our energy and life from the change that happens produced by the Holy Spirit.

Gazing on His Wounds

In Eucharistic adoration we gaze upon the wounds of Jesus. "They shall look upon him whom they have pierced" (Jn 19:37). If we make a habit of this way of praying, we will find that we are dwelling often on the mystery of his passion. We are "wounded" with love, aroused in a desire for union with Jesus, ready to forsake everything for that one goal of being with him completely. His love pierces our hearts and opens them with a burning desire for him. He creates in us a desire for union, and at the same time an awareness of our utter incapacity to attain this union. "The love of Christ overwhelms us ..." (2 Cor 5:14). We are persuaded by the fire of his love. His perfect love wins our hearts, and becomes a consuming fire. We want him so much! And yet we know we are still so hard, cold and indifferent, tepid and apathetic! In the depths of our hearts there are deep roots of sin that need purification. We give him permission to penetrate our hearts with his love, and slowly we become more like him. Over time we discover a change is taking place. We have a new power to love him and to love others.

Down through the ages prayerful men and women have contemplated the five wounds of Jesus. St Bonaventure was to sum up this contemplative gaze, "Through the visible wounds we see the wounds of invisible love."[80] This spiritual experience of the loving mercy of Christ was awakened more profoundly by Bernard of Clairvaux who interpreted the Song of Songs in terms of the love of God made visible in the pierced heart of Christ:

> The secret of his heart is laid bare in the wounds of his body. One can easily read in them the mystery of God's infinite goodness and merciful tenderness which came down to us like a dawning from on high. How, Lord, could you show more clearly than by your wounds that you are indeed full of goodness and mercy, abounding in love?[81]

Francis of Assisi had such a deep love for the wounds of Jesus, and for the internal suffering of Jesus on the cross, that he was granted the stigmata in his body. Others such as St Gertrude and St Mechtilde experienced in prayer the phenomenon of an exchange of hearts. All of this led towards the experience of Margaret Mary Alacoque, a Sister of the Visitation, an order founded by Francis de Sales. On the feast of John the evangelist in 1673, while praying before the Blessed Sacrament she experienced the divine heart of Jesus madly on fire with love for all men and women. This fire of love was so powerful that it could not be contained. Jesus asked for her heart, and she gave it to him. He took it and placed it in the furnace of his own heart. She said it seemed "like a tiny atom being consumed in that blazing furnace".[82] When he drew her heart out of the furnace and placed it back into her chest she knew the searing of love, the piercing of her own heart with divine love for the world.

The same sort of powerful transformation that Margaret Mary Alacoque experienced mystically is intended for each one of us. It happens over time and usually not in the dramatic fashion that Margaret Mary experienced. God's purpose is to draw us into the fire of love in the heart of Christ for us, and for the whole world. If we are open and come with faith then Jesus will touch us in the depth of our being with the love of God which is beyond all telling. "We are the ones who put our faith in God's love for us." (1 Jn 4)

Solitude in the Desert

This Eucharistic love inflamed the heart of Blessed Charles de Foucauld. After living a dissolute life in France as a young man, given to the pleasures of the world, his conversion began when he was impressed by the intense faith of Muslims in Algiers where he was serving in the French Foreign Legion. This lead him on a search for God. When back in Paris he was surprisingly challenged by a priest to humble himself and repent, he received the grace to do so. He related that having received absolution he knew beyond doubt that God did exist, and now the only response he could make was to give over his whole life to the Lord. After a time in a Trappist monastery he was drawn to seek Jesus in the humility of Nazareth. Working as a common gardener for Poor Clare sisters he would spend hours in their chapel kneeling with love before the Blessed Sacrament. After eventually becoming a priest he felt called to live in the remotest regions of the Sahara desert, as a witness of love amongst the most abandoned people. He would keep silent vigil at nights in the little chapel in his humble dwelling, pouring out his heart to his Beloved: "You are there, my Lord Jesus, in the Holy Eucharist. You are there but a few feet from me, in the tabernacle. Your body, your soul, your humanity, your divinity, your entire being is there in its double nature! How close you are, God!"[83] He saw the presence of Jesus in the Blessed Sacrament to be so real, that he sensed rays of love radiating out towards the whole surrounding area.

The loving intimacy spent in adoration at the feet of the one he loved prompted him to go out towards the least of his brothers and sisters. He identified with Jesus in love for the most abandoned of all. He lived as the only priest, the only Christian, amongst the Tuareg people, who accepted him as a "holy man" even though not of their faith. For Charles, serving Christ in the Sacrament and serving Christ in the poor was the one act of worship. His heart was glued to the Blessed Sacrament. In the depths of the night, with no Christian within hundreds of miles, he relished intimacy with Christ. He wrote in his diary:

> How sweet they are, these hours of the night! ... All is silent outside, all is sleeping. The darkness envelops all being, and you permit me to stay awake at your feet, so that I alone in this death of nature am living for you. My Beloved, when all slumbers, how sweet it is to tell you that we love you, that we wish to live for you alone.[84]

Come to Me all you who Labour

Jim, a married man in his forties, had become heavily burdened emotionally due to his two drug-affected children, who were still living in the family home. His wife was very supportive, but the situation was testing their capacity to cope. Both Jim and his wife are very committed in their Catholic faith. Jim decided to undertake an eight day silent retreat. He says, "I felt completely destroyed interiorly and commenced the retreat with little expectation or hope in my heart." Jim found he wasn't able to do the exercises that were asked of him by the retreat director. He was so burdened by intense pain, anger and confusion, that all he felt he could do was to simply sit for hours before the Blessed Sacrament. Towards the end of the retreat Jim became aware of what he called later "an interior sunrise dawning". Alone in adoration before the Blessed Sacrament he knew a healing was happening. "I felt completely whole and integrated at the core of my being, and a deep peace and stillness that nothing could disturb or take away." Jim lives joyfully now from this restoration experience, which he calls his own "transfiguration" encounter.

Adoration is also a wonderful antidote to the poison of sin. The people of Israel had grumbled against God. As a result they were afflicted with poisonous snakes biting them and endangering their lives. Moses cried out to God. He was told to fashion a bronze serpent. All who were bitten, if they looked at the bronze serpent would be healed. In the gospel Jesus identifies himself with this symbol of the bronze serpent. "When I am lifted up from the earth I will draw all to myself." When we are afflicted by lustful images, prideful thoughts, unruly anger, envious feelings, or any other poison of the soul, we need to rush to the Blessed Sacrament, gaze upon the host, and let the healing come, which can only be ministered by the touch of Jesus. But it is not magic. It is the transforming power of love. When we are perilously afflicted by temptations, rather than try to analyse or rationalise what is happening, run quickly to the Blessed Sacrament and cling to Jesus. Just as the woman with the haemorrhage touched the hem of his cloak, cling to the Lord, and over time allow the power of his healing to flow through you.

It is simply a matter of being in the presence of Jesus. We don't have to do much; no fancy prayers or devotional exercises are necessary. His presence is warm, welcoming, accepting and healing. We come as we are with all the hurts and bruises, the set-backs and disappointments, the pain and the struggle of life. We find shelter from the storm, comfort in affliction. We don't really have to say anything; nor do we need to hear any words from Jesus. It is enough to be there in his presence. We always go away lifted in spirit, strengthened for the journey, and encouraged to face the battle with a new-found hope.

Communal Adoration

Eucharistic adoration can be personal or communal. When it is communal we worship together, singing, praising, standing or kneeling, whatever the Holy Spirit inspires us to do. The risen Jesus is in our midst. We may use the normal ritual for Benediction, or some variation on it. We have found it is powerful when the priest carries the exposed Blessed Sacrament in the monstrance through the assembly as the people kneel and adore the Lord, reaching out in their hearts to touch him, believing in his healing presence with us. These can be times when the Lord in his mercy brings a healing. A communal Holy Hour is often a beautiful time when the full force of the magnificence of the risen Christ present before us becomes more evident, and the faith of the people is set on fire. Mother Teresa once said, "When you look at the Crucifix you understand how much Jesus loved you then. When you look at the sacred host you understand how much Jesus loves you *now*."

PART V

MISSION

Our communities, when they celebrate the Eucharist, must become ever more conscious that the sacrifice of Christ is for all, and that the Eucharist thus compels all who believe in him to become 'bread that is broken' for others, and to work for the building of a more just and fraternal world ... Each of us is truly called together with Jesus to be bread broken for the life of the world. (Pope Benedict, SC 88)

God in Christ was reconciling the world to himself ... and he has entrusted to us the news that they are reconciled. So we are ambassadors for Christ; it is as though God were appealing through us, and the appeal that we make in Christ's name is: be reconciled to God. (2 Cor 5:19-20)

15

PROCLAIMING THE GOOD NEWS

"As often as you eat this bread and drink this cup, you proclaim the death of the Lord until he comes." (1 Cor 11:26)

Missionary Disciples

Eucharist by definition is the joyful proclamation of Jesus crucified until he comes again. It is a profoundly evangelical reality, as is the Church who celebrates it. The Eucharist is a word-event in which the crucified and risen Christ is made present for all. This is the sacrament that makes present the sacrifice of Jesus given for the salvation of the world. It is directed outwards to all men and women. In the Eucharistic prayer we pray that the fruits of the sacrifice will be experienced by all, but then we move out as a people to actively bring this gift of salvation to as many as possible. At the end of the Mass the celebrant in the name of Jesus and his church sends the participants forward with the words, *"Ite missa est"*, "go you are sent". The name Mass (*Missa*) is taken from this dismissal formula. We are the people who are "sent". Jesus said to his apostles on Easter morning, "As the Father has sent me, so I am sending you!" Another possible dismissal the priest can use is, "Go, and announce the gospel of the Lord!" Everything is geared towards joyfully going forth, preaching the good news that we have a loving Saviour who has redeemed us and is our hope. As Pope Benedict has reminded us, "we cannot approach the Eucharistic table without being drawn into mission, which beginning with the very heart of God, is meant to reach all people".[85]

The Eucharist is the source and summit of the Church's mission. The Church exists to evangelise. This is its deepest identity.[86] When we celebrate Eucharist we are expressing who we are as a people and we are seeking to become more deeply who we are. An authentic Eucharistic Church is a missionary Church. It is simply a matter of being true to ourselves. Pope Francis dreams of a Church which is living this reality, a community of "missionary disciples" which goes forth into the world joyfully proclaiming the good news of Jesus.[87]

In the Eucharist we experience a profound personal encounter with the risen Christ still carrying his wounds. There is nothing more beautiful for the human heart than to be surprised again by the power of God's word proclaimed in the Eucharist and through receiving the incarnate Word himself in Holy Communion. This living encounter with Jesus impels us to share joyfully with others the light, hope, and freedom which he brings to human hearts. We will do this firstly through the witness of our lives, but then also by the words the Spirit prompts us to speak, words which touch the hearts of others because they come from the Lord himself. As Pope Benedict observes, "The more ardent the love for the Eucharist in the hearts of the Christian people, the more clearly will they recognise the goal of all mission: *to bring Christ to others.*"[88]

An Evangelising Community

In this endeavour to evangelise we can't underestimate the importance of a vibrant community of faith and love which provides a welcoming presence, a place of acceptance and healing. The truly Eucharistic community offers a home; a sense of belonging to the many who are lost, abandoned and confused, without any meaning or goal in life. It shares the hospitality in the heart of God and always has an open door for those who have become estranged and alienated from the Father's house. A genuine Eucharistic community will shine resplendently with the merciful face of Christ, so that those who have fallen away, or maybe fallen into self-destructive patterns of living, can find their way home. An evocative image of the Church used by Pope Francis likens it to a "field hospital after a battle". The real need is compassion and healing, rather than judgement and condemnation.

Yet while we must have the home lights burning, we also need to be a people who will go out after the straying sheep. The genuine Eucharistic community will not be focussed inwards, attending only to its internal problems, jealous about its structures and practices. As Pope Francis has famously said, "I prefer a Church which is bruised, hurting and dirty because it has been out on the streets, rather than a Church which is unhealthy from being confined and from clinging to its own security."[89] People are starving for the bread of life, for the food for their souls. We who feed often on the word of God and the body and blood of the Lord cannot remain in our Church buildings waiting for people to come. We need to find creative alternative strategies for bringing the good news of Jesus to those who would never darken the door of a Church, except maybe for a baptism, wedding or funeral. We need to find a way of building bridges from the secularised cultural milieu that most people live in and find a way of leading them towards the Bread of Life.

A Whole Process

It is helpful to be able to position the actual Eucharistic celebration within the overall process of evangelisation. If we were to draw up a rather stylised pattern of the way a person is evangelised, we could identify four stages. Firstly, a time of initial evangelisation which is achieved largely through individual witness of members of the community who are on fire with the love of Jesus, living closely with people and involved in their daily lives, full of compassion and ready to listen to the heart-aches they have, supporting them in practical ways and encouraging them in initial steps of faith. At this stage the witness of the community itself is crucial. It is simply a matter of saying to a friend, "Come and See!" with confidence they will discover a new way of life witnessed in the relationships and the manner of living of the Christian community. The second phase is the time of being soaked in the proclaimed word of God which is aiming towards conversion of heart. Here it is crucial that the new-comer hears the *kerygma* preached, the fundamental proclamation of the saving love of God made visible in Jesus crucified. If they are coming to Mass they will hopefully hear *kerygmatic* preaching, but there may be other contexts, such as a home-based prayer meeting, an organised rally, or a weekend set aside for this purpose. As Paul says, "Faith comes from what is preached, and what is preached comes from the word of Christ." (Rom 10:17)

In the third phase the person is ideally guided in a one to one relationship with one of the members of the community. This is a time of deepening in personal conversion to Jesus. Having responded to the gospel message the person has encountered Jesus as Saviour and Lord and is now developing in a personal relationship with Jesus through the scriptures and other sources of feeding for personal consolation and enlightenment. The new disciple is also being initiated into the sacramental life of the Church, or deepened in what had been left to lapse. It is a time of being fully incorporated into the Church. At this stage the Eucharist comes more powerfully into play. The person needs to know more about the meaning and purpose of the Eucharist and learn how to consciously and actively participate in the celebration. He or she will also discover the wonder of Eucharistic adoration.

Until this point the whole movement has been heading towards the Eucharist as the summit of the person's newly enlivened faith. But evangelisation does not finish there. All along the way of evangelical Catholic formation this newly formed disciple needs to be encouraged to become involved in apostolic activity. Even though freshly alive to the wonder of the risen Christ, the excitement, joy and enthusiasm of this discovery will hopefully impel the new disciple to share this joy with others. The fourth and final stage of evangelisation is to train the newcomer specifically in how to evangelise, how best to meet others and share with them the good news of Jesus in a non-threatening and attractive manner. At this point the daily food of the Eucharist and regular periods of adoration of Jesus in the Blessed Sacrament provide a fire within the heart, a love that propels them forward to share this gift with others. As Paul VI observed, "Here lies the test of truth, the touchstone of evangelisation ... that the person who has been evangelised goes on to evangelise others."[90]

Eucharist: an Evangelising Event

This phased approach to evangelisation helps us understand the overall dynamic, but I would not want to convey the impression that the Eucharist is only important in the third and fourth phase. Actually that was the case in the early post-apostolic Church. The early Christians kept secret what happened in the Eucharist until people were initiated into the sacraments. The sacred mysteries were understood to be so holy that they should not be profaned by pagan presence. That only fuelled rumours amongst the pagans that Christians were engaged in "human sacrifices" or "cannibalism". In today's world we could well do with a touch of that reverence of the early years, but our context for evangelisation is necessarily different. It almost always involves the Eucharist in some way. We invite the uninitiated to our communities, and the high point of our communion is when we gather around the table of the Lord. So from the beginning of the evangelising process we are engaging people in the Mass. If the Mass is noted for its Spirit-filled preaching that is relevant to the lives of the listeners, and heartfelt worship assisted by an inspired music ministry, it can be an evangelising event itself. Add to this a community with a heart of hospitality, and openness to all the various gifts of the Spirit being exercised by the laity, and we can be confident that new-comers will be evangelised. The Eucharistic celebration itself can be a profound means of on-going evangelisation.

The problem arises if the local Catholic community is made up of "consumers" rather that disciples and apostles. We live in a consumer society, where people are not satisfied for long with what they have, and are taught that there is always around the corner a new commodity to fill their unmet needs. The consumer mentality can spell death to a faith community. They are thinking first of themselves and meeting their felt needs. This attitude means they can be demanding in their expectations of what should be given to them at Mass, but with little or no commitment to build the community or to reach out to newcomers. The Eucharist is "for me", and if I am not satisfied in this parish then I will go and find a better one. I will go "where I am fed". Consumer Catholics can be very critical of the local community but not be prepared to lift a finger to help make things better. Even when they are blessed with a new, rich and exciting experience of Eucharist, they will stick around as grateful receivers, but not as willing givers.

An evangelising community thinks differently. It builds a culture where those who are inside the Church are always thinking of those outside, and gear the whole experience of the Sunday Eucharist to welcome the newcomers.[91] The community is primarily made up of disciples of Jesus, who really want to share the "infinite treasure of Christ" with as many as possible. They are not thinking of "what I can get out of this", but rather of "how I can help others discover this wonderful mystery". And surprisingly the more they welcome and serve the newcomer the more they find they are enriched themselves.

16

HEALING POWER

> "He took our infirmities and bore our diseases ... by his wounds we are healed." (Is 53:4-5)

To Touch Jesus

Jesus sent his apostles "to proclaim the kingdom of God and to heal" (Lk 9:2). The evangelising ministry of Jesus included both preaching the word and healing ministry. This healing power of Jesus continues in the Church today. In the Mass we meet Jesus in the word proclaimed that will cleanse, heal and free us. We are deepened in faith, and called to conversion, which opens us more to be able to receive the healing power of the Lord. Just like those in the gospels who were healed through faith when they encountered Jesus, so also are we in the Eucharist. The leper who approached Jesus on his knees, pleading "If you want to, you can heal me" heard Jesus reply, "Of course I want to. Be cured." This is the assurance of Jesus for each one of us as we come to the Eucharistic celebration. In the Mass we are reliving the sacrifice of Jesus on Calvary, which was sufficient to cleanse, heal and bring redemption to the world. His salvific power includes the grace for healing of the whole person, body, mind, emotions and spirit. He is now the risen Lord, but he is still carrying his wounds, and it is "by his wounds" we shall be healed. Nothing should hold us back from turning our hearts towards Jesus for healing.

In the gospels we have the story of the woman who had a haemorrhage for twelve years and had gone to many doctors with no satisfaction (Mk 5:25-34). She pressed through the crowd, desperate to touch Jesus. She was thinking to herself, "Even if I touch the fringe of his cloak I will be well again." Jesus stopped. He felt the power go out from him. "Who touched me?" His disciples were puzzled. There was a whole crowd jostling around him. Many people were touching him. But Jesus continued to look around for the one person in the crowd who had touched him with faith. This touch of faith had drawn the healing power; she had been healed instantly. Now she was at his feet admitting what she had done, fearful of reproach, because touching Jesus would have rendered him ritually impure. But he was not worried about that. He simply wanted to encourage her, "Your faith has saved you; go in peace, free from your distress."

This woman's attitude is a model for us as we enter into the Eucharist. We come with all our complaints. The woman had a physical issue, but accompanying this would have been the deep emotional wounding of being in that society isolated from others and ostracised because of her condition. She would have been burdened with a low self-image and a deep sense of rejection, possibly carrying much self-pity, but not enough to stop her from vigorously seeking the healing of the Lord. Whatever our own struggle, whether it is physical illness, or interior distress, we are guaranteed the healing touch of Jesus in the Eucharist. Before receiving Holy Communion we say in response to the priest's invitation, "Lord I am not worthy that you should enter under my roof, but only say the word and my soul shall be healed." These are the words of the centurion in the gospel who was beseeching Jesus to heal his servant. Jesus said, "Not even in Israel have I found faith like this." The servant was healed at that moment. How wonderful that we actually receive Christ who is the Healer into our bodies in Holy Communion. We believe that he will heal us. When in the liturgy we express our faith that "my soul will be healed", we really mean healing for the whole person, soul, mind and body.

Healing of Mind and Body

A woman gave testimony that she was praying for her husband whose addiction to gambling was causing financial problems, but also putting a major stress on the marriage. One day at Mass quite unexpectedly she felt inspired to ask God "if he felt the time was right for me to have a baby". She let the Lord know that if he thought the time was right it would be OK with her. But she added the proviso, "You will have to look after me." She felt her problems were bad enough already, and was fearful that having a child would make it worse. But she was willing to entrust herself and her whole future to God. She was able to surrender all her anxieties to the Lord. Well, everything changed with that decision. The child was born, and a proud father was reborn. Peace has come to the house, and he has become a caring, supportive and hard working husband ever since.

Sr. Briege McKenna tells the following story.[92] A woman who was suffering from a stomach cancer had been told by the doctors that there was no point in operating because it had spread so extensively. Her stomach was distended because of the size of the tumour. But her deeper problem was a chronic fear of dying. When she came to ask for healing prayer she was pleading that God would take away this awful fear of death. Sister said to her, "Go to meet Jesus in the Eucharist ... Jesus will supply you with the strength to face whatever is on your road of life. If he is going to bring you through the door of death he will give you the grace to go through that door without this awful fear. And if you are to live, he will give you the grace to live."

The woman did as she was advised. She went to Mass, and when she was walking up to communion she said to herself, "In a few minutes I am going to meet Jesus ... I will ask him for his help." So when she took the sacred host in her hand she said to the Lord, "I know you are really here. When you come into me take away this fear. Heal me if you want to, but please do something for me." She said later, "I had no sooner put the host on my tongue and swallowed it than I felt as though something was burning in my throat and down into my stomach. I looked down at my stomach and the growth was gone."

Sign of Deeper Change

In the gospels physical healings are always a sign of the kingdom of God taking hold in our lives. They are intended to lead us to repentance of sin and deeper conversion of heart. When Jesus healed the paralysed man, who had been lowered down through the roof, his first words to the man were, "Your sins are forgiven you" (Mk 2:1-12). When the Pharisees questioned his power to forgive sins, Jesus replied, "Which is easier to say 'your sins are forgiven' or 'stand up and walk'? To prove to you that the Son of Man has the power to forgive sins" he said to the paralytic, "I order you; get up, pick up your stretcher and walk." And the man got up and walked out in front of them all. The physical healing was clearly a demonstration that the kingdom of God, which brings peace through forgiveness of sins, was taking hold before their very eyes.

This next testimony of Jesus healing through the Eucharist illustrates this point. When the Lord heals someone his saving action reaches very deep, and gives rise to a repentant heart; and he heals the worst disease of all – sin. Fr. Emilien Tardiff told this story.[93] A 34-year-old Belgian man who had been living a sinful life was suffering from cancer in the right foot. The cancer was in an advanced state and its effects were clearly visible on his foot. The doctors wanted to amputate the leg but the man refused. The stricken man heard about a healing Mass being celebrated, and he decided to attend. During the Mass, and the prayers for healing, he felt an intense heat in his right foot, as if it was near a fire. He felt different, but wasn't sure why. That night for the first time in years he slept without sleeping pills. The next morning he realised that the pain had gone from his foot. When they removed the bandage from the foot they discovered to their delight that it was perfectly healthy. There were no sores; the tissues had been restored. Jumping for joy the man rushed to the clinic to tell the doctors. They were atheists, and they were bewildered because they could not explain what had happened. The young man told them, "The Lord healed me yesterday during the Eucharist."

The young man realised that Jesus is alive and present in the Eucharist. He is the same Jesus who raised Lazarus from the dead, and who healed many people who were lame and crippled, and many who were deaf and blind. As he began to reflect on his life the young man was confronted with the sin that had a grip on his heart. The Lord gave him the grace to repent and to renounce his sin, and to walk in the way of a disciple, sharing in fullness of life from Jesus. Not long afterwards he entered a seminary. As the Lord had healed him through the Eucharist he wanted to come as close as possible to that mystery and eventually to celebrate it himself one day. He is now a priest in a contemplative order, each day celebrating the mystery of faith in which we announce the death of the Lord until he comes, and profess our faith that Jesus is risen and alive and that he is Lord of all.

The Decision to Forgive

One of the main obstacles preventing us from receiving the healing power of Jesus is resentment, bitterness of heart, a refusal to forgive. This is a deep sickness of the heart which can divide communities and prevent the grace of the Eucharist to flow freely. The Eucharist is a sacrament of forgiveness of sins, helping us to know we are forgiven by God, and making us ready to forgive others. Yet stubborn resentment can frustrate this grace from being effective. Because of past hurts we can be holding up a clenched fist within our hearts against another person or group of people who have offended us. The Eucharistic liturgy begins with a confession of faults and an act of confidence in the mercy of God. This is a good place to make the decision to forgive. It is an act of the will under God's grace. Feelings may be chaotic, but the grace is always there to choose to forgive. Sometimes the grace to forgive comes during the liturgy of the word, especially if the preaching happens to be directed that way. We can bring all the hurt and pain of our lives to the wounded heart of Jesus. We can join our prayer of forgiveness with his, when he was being nailed to the cross, "Father, forgive them, for they know not what they do." This grace of being able to forgive liberates us. We discover that our resentment had been like a cancer that has now been dissolved. Although we had wished the worst for the offender, in fact our hatred and resentment had been the worst form of imprisonment for ourselves.

Sometimes the hatred in our hearts can be so deep that we are not fully conscious of it, but it detrimentally affects our lives. Clyde Cook was an Australian soldier fighting the Japanese on the Kokoda trail in Papua New Guinea.[94] He had lost his best mate, and six of his platoon, that had been ambushed when he was in command. He blamed himself and hated the Japanese. On honourable discharge from the Army due to injuries, he married the woman who had nursed him to health. He still carried inside himself the deep hurt and resentment. Providentially, one day he picked up a book on healing. Reading this book brought him into intense emotional confusion, and he thought he was going out of his mind. His wife invited him to a healing retreat, and he had the opportunity of prayer for healing. After this he felt liberated and supposed all was well. Some years later Clyde was invited to take part in a Mass celebrating reconciliation between

Australians and Japanese. A pilgrimage of 32 Japanese war widows was to attend the Mass to be held in a retreat house in Brisbane.

The night before the Mass Clyde went with the priest into the chapel. He had a fierce reaction inside himself. The Japanese war-flag had been erected near the altar. Lying beside it was a Japanese samurai sword. Then, to make matters worse, the priest stunned Clyde by asking him to carry the Japanese flag in the Offertory procession the next day. Two Japanese war widows would carry up icons of Mary and the child Jesus. Clyde was full of horror and revulsion. That night he struggled with anger, fear, hatred and depression. In the middle of the night he desperately called out to Jesus. He sensed the Lord giving him a choice; continue to hate the Japanese or decide to be a disciple. Clyde decided to be a disciple. In the middle of the night he penned a letter to the 32 Japanese pilgrims, which he intended to give them the next day. He relates:

> I found myself confessing to them that I had hated them, and why. But now I knew I was wrong, and I no longer hated them. I told them I would join the two widows in the Offertory procession, and make it a real Mass, in memory of His bloodshed and death, a real re-presentation of the wounded, bleeding, dying Jesus. His bloody sacrifice took in all the pain and bleeding and dying that happened in the horrible jungle warfare. His dying gave meaning to all the deaths because He showed in His own body that there can be a resurrection to eternal life.

17

SHARING IN THE VICTORY OF JESUS

"Do not be afraid; I am the first and the last, and the living one. I was dead, and see, I am alive forever and ever; and I have the key of Death and of Hades." (Rev 1:17-18)

Victory over Sin

In the Eucharist we share in the victory of Jesus over sin, death and Satan. The victory of Jesus over sin was won by his offering of himself in our place on the cross. "God made the sinless one into sin, so that in him we might become the righteousness of God" (2 Cor 5:21). In solidarity with us on the cross, Jesus bore the full consequences of our sin, which had separated us from God. And from that pit of darkness he made the perfect act of love and obedience to the Father, which has won our redemption. He entered fully into our wounded human condition. Being one with us he turned our slavery due to sin into the freedom and victory of the sons and daughters of God. Now that he is risen from the dead the power of his redemption can be experienced in our lives. The Eucharist is a powerful moment when we are reinforced in this victory over sin. Every Eucharist deepens us in the graces of Baptism. Paul tells us that when we were baptised we were joined with Jesus in his death. It is as if we went into the tomb with him. But Jesus was raised from the dead by the Father. So in Baptism we too were joined with Jesus in resurrection. He says, "We know that our old self was crucified with him so that the body of sin might be destroyed, and we might no longer be enslaved to sin." (Rom 6:6)

It is not fully clear what Paul means by this "body of sin", but I suggest he is referring to the strong patterns of sin that have a hold on our hearts; the grooves of the "old self" which need to be broken. We can feel overwhelmed by the sinful habits and addictions, thoughts and actions that recur again and again, which we don't seem to be able to control. We feel dominated by these forces of sin within us and seem to have no way out of our predicament. Consequently, we live without hope, a feeling of oppression upon our souls, living in a down-hearted and defeated manner, rather than as sons and daughters of God. The good news is that by the grace of our Baptism we can overcome this debilitating effect of sin. But the reality is that for most of us we have not yet fully appropriated this baptismal gift.

Every time we celebrate Eucharist we can make a deeper "yes" to Christ's redeeming power made present and active for us by the Holy Spirit. We are immersed more into the death and resurrection of Jesus. We more deeply take hold of the victory won for us by Jesus. As Paul says, "When Christ died, he died once and for all, to sin, so his life now is life with God; and in that way you too must consider yourselves to be dead to sin and alive for God in Christ Jesus" (Rom 6:11). Offering ourselves, broken as we are, with all our sinful attitudes and behaviour, and bringing our wounded selves to the cross of Jesus, we find healing and deliverance. Partaking of the body and blood of Jesus we gain forgiveness for our lesser sins and gain new strength to break the patterns that continue to enslave us.

Victory over Death

Eucharist also helps us share in Christ's victory over death. As we have already indicated, we triumph over the "spiritual" death, which comes as the "wages of sin". But Eucharist is also a wonderful victory over the otherwise threatening experience of "bodily" death, whenever our pilgrim journey here on earth will come to an end. This is why it is most appropriate to have a Requiem Mass for a funeral. The Eucharist is a "pledge of future glory". Jesus promises, "Those who eat my flesh and drink my blood have eternal life, and I will raise them up on the last day" (Jn 6:54). The flesh of Christ which we eat in the Eucharist is the glorious body of the risen Christ. Consequently we are guaranteed of being bodily raised with him on the last day. The Eucharist is the banquet of eternal life, already a foretaste of what is yet to come in the wedding feast of the Lamb. Christian funerals are full of hope as we rejoice in the risen Christ, no matter what the tragic circumstances of the death. In the light of his resurrection faith Paul cries out "Death has been swallowed up on victory. Where, O death, is your victory? Where, O death, is your sting?" (1 Cor 15:56). He gives thanks to God "who gives us the victory through our Lord Jesus Christ." According to Paul, the resurrection of Christ is the "first fruits of those who have died". If we die in Christ we shall live in him forever. Christ's resurrection is the pattern for our own glorious resurrection in him.

For many of our contemporaries death is a black hole of nothingness, a journey into oblivion, or maybe an existence similar to that of *sheol*, "the land of shadows" in the Old Testament. When we celebrate Eucharist we are steeped in a different perspective. Eucharist is a foretaste of the fullness of joy promised by Christ. The purpose of Christ's loving gift of himself is so that we would "remain in his love". Jesus said, "I have told you this so that my own joy may be in you and your joy complete" (Jn 15:11). He is our lasting joy, the fullness of life now, and forever. St Ignatius of Antioch called the Eucharistic bread "a medicine of immortality, an antidote to death, and the food that makes us live forever in Christ Jesus".[95]

Celebrating Eucharist we confidently await the "blessed hope and the coming of our Saviour Jesus Christ".[96] In the Mass as we strain forward to the great and awesome day when Christ will come again in glory, we already experience a touch of heaven now. The priest calls the people to "lift up your hearts" and the people reply "we lift them up to the Lord". Together we lift up our hearts to the vision of the heavenly liturgy with all the angels and saints worshipping around the throne of the Lamb. We participate in the heavenly liturgy. As the Catechism explains:

> In the earthly liturgy we share in a foretaste of that heavenly liturgy which is celebrated in the Holy City of Jerusalem toward which we journey as pilgrims, where Christ is sitting at the right hand of God, minister of the sanctuary and of the true tabernacle. With all the warriors of the heavenly army we sing a hymn of glory to the Lord; venerating the memory of the saints, we hope for some part and fellowship with them; we eagerly await the Saviour, our Lord Jesus Christ, until he, our life, shall appear and we too will appear with him in glory.[97]

When celebrating the Eucharist we are already sharing in the heavenly liturgy. The Mass is a touch of "heaven on earth".

Victory over Satan

In the Eucharist we also share in the victory of Christ over Satan and all powers of evil and darkness. We are sharing in the victory already won by the Christ when he was "lifted up" on the cross for our sake, and then "lifted up" by the Father in resurrection and ascension. When his "hour" had come, Jesus foretold this victory, "Now sentence is being passed on this world; now the prince of this world (Satan) is to be overthrown. And when I am lifted up from the earth I shall draw all to myself" (Jn 12:31-32). In Eucharist we share in this "hour" of victory. When the people of Israel passed through the Red Sea dry shod, and the pursuing Egyptian army was destroyed, Moses let out a mighty roar of victory. "I will sing to the Lord for he has triumphed gloriously; horse and rider he has thrown into the sea. The Lord is my strength and my might, and he has become my salvation ... The Lord is a warrior, the Lord is his name" (Ex 15:1-2, 3-4). Every time we celebrate the Mass we let out a cry of victory also. Christ our Saviour has delivered us from the power of Satan. He has crushed our ancient enemy and all his minions.

Once a young man came to me who obviously was a victim to strongholds of Satan in his life due to destructive sinful patterns. There were areas of besetting sin by which he had allowed evil spirits unwanted access. He was experiencing bondage in these areas. I promised to pray deliverance prayer with him the following week, but strongly advised him to go to Mass every day until our appointment. He did this faithfully. When he arrived the next week I could see there was an obvious change in his appearance and demeanour. He exuded peace and joy. After talking with him for some time I realised that the Lord had already delivered him. The power of the Eucharist was enough. There was nothing else I needed to do but to pray for the infilling of the Holy Spirit and to encourage him to keep going to Mass.

Jesus has won the conclusive victory over Satan. "It was to undo all that the devil has done that the Son of God appeared" (1 Jn 3:8). Paul says, "He disarmed the rulers and authorities, and paraded them in public, behind him in his triumphal procession" (Col 2:15). The image here is of captive enemy soldiers being stripped of their arms and paraded in public as they were led back to Rome in chains, a dismal procession behind the triumphant general. That is how Christ the victor has dealt with his enemies. The risen Christ reigns. He has put all of his enemies under his feet. In Eucharist we are clothed with this resurrection power of God. Paul says, "God put this power to work in Christ when he raised him from the dead and seated him at his right hand in the heavenly places, far above all rule and authority and power and dominion, and above every name that is named ... And he has put all things under his feet and has made him head over all things ..." (Eph 1:20-22)

Victory already won; Battle will be won

Celebrating Eucharist we remember what Jesus through his death and resurrection has done for us. But we also anticipate the complete victory in heaven. The Eucharist helps us be aware that even though the battle with Satan and evil spirits still rages, the decisive victory has *already been won*. And, further to this, the on-going battle that we must fight now *will be won in the end*. We know we have the Blessed Virgin Mary and all the saints and angels on our side. The Mass anticipates the heavenly victory; it brings heaven on earth. We are caught up in the victory song of the saints and martyrs, "Alleluia! The reign of the Lord God Almighty has begun; let us be glad and joyful and give praise to God, because this is the time for the marriage of the Lamb" (Rev 19:7).

In every Eucharistic celebration, no matter how simple and humble the circumstances, the heavens open, and we are caught up in the victorious praise and worship of all those who have already fully attained their salvation. *Revelations* tells us there is a huge number which is impossible to count, people from every nation, race, tribe and language. All are "standing in front of the Lamb, dressed in white robes and holding palms in their hands" and they are shouting loudly, "Victory to our God, who sits on the throne, and to the Lamb!" They are prostrating themselves before the Lamb on the throne as they worship God, "Amen, Praise and glory and wisdom and thanksgiving and honour and power and strength to our God forever and ever. Amen" (Rev 7:9-12). With all of heaven on our side what have we to fear?

In the spiritual battle the best armour of God is daily Eucharist. The gates of hell will not prevail against the Church. In the sacrifice of the Mass history achieves its goal. Christ, the Lamb of God, and the Church, his bride, celebrate their wedding feast and consummate their marriage. Christ is the Alpha and the Omega, the beginning and the end of all history. The event of Calvary, the death of Jesus on the cross, is the centre point and the hinge of all history. The whole redeeming power of his death and resurrection is contained in this sacrament. The Mass also anticipates the end of all history, the second coming of the Lord. There is no moment in all history more powerful than the Eucharistic worship. All heaven is on our side. Before this array of heavenly Spirit-filled warriors the devil is impotent and flees.

We have nothing to fear of Satan. The manifestations of consummate evil in our present age should not deter us from our goal. In the midst of all the atrocities and human calamities of our time we cannot lose hope. We touch into the new Jerusalem in the Mass; the Spirit and the bride say, "Come, Lord Jesus!" Come Jesus and assume your kingship; come and manifest your reign. We join the angels and saints singing, "Holy, holy, holy" With all the hosts of angels and archangels, and with all the heavenly company, we sing to the praise and glory of God. The word "hosts" has been highlighted in the new translation of the Mass. It has connotation of military might – the "legions" of angels and saints. The Mass engages us in the battle. We proclaim that God is our fortress and our strength. When we receive Holy Communion it is like eating fire. The evil spirits are driven out, we are cleansed of our sin, and are given a new capacity to be watchful over the heart to guard it from any incursions of the powers of darkness.

Eucharist Stronger than All the Evil in the World

Sometimes the blatant evil in our age can be oppressive and tempt us to lose hope for the world - the drug cartels in Mexico, the Mafia in Italy, the wanton bloodshed of Islamic extremists, the carnage of numerous wars, the increasing threat of terrorism, the degradation of human trafficking and child slavery – all these human tragedies which seem so dark and sinister, orchestrated by the power of Satan. But all is not as it seems. History has been redeemed by Jesus Christ. We live in the time when the Kingdom of God is already taking hold, and have a sure guarantee of its completion. Pope John Paul II reminded us that by entering into the Saviour's sacrificial offering we already share in the victory won by him over all the evil in the world. This victory is to be appropriated by us now, and from its power we will confidently build a new civilisation of life and love. In particular the Eucharist is central to this gift and task:

> When we are shaken by the sight of evil spreading in the universe, with all the devastation which it produces, we should not forget that such unleashing of the forces of sin is overcome by the saving power of Christ. Whenever the words of consecration are uttered in the Mass and the body and blood of Christ become present in the act of sacrifice, the triumph of love over hatred, of holiness over sin, is also present. Every Eucharistic celebration is stronger than all the evil in the universe; it means real, concrete accomplishment of the redemption, and ever deeper reconciliation of sinful man with God, in prospect of a better world.[98]

18

INTERCESSION

"Ask and it will be given to you; search and you will find; knock, and the door will be opened." (Lk 11:9)

The Powerful Prayer of Jesus

The Eucharist is the Church's most powerful prayer of intercession. This is because the sacrifice which Jesus offered on the cross is now eternal. He lives forever as the one mediator between God and man. All intercessory prayer is effective because of Jesus. The Church's prayer in the Eucharist makes present this perfect prayer of Christ to the Father, which he uttered on the cross, and now continues on our behalf seated in glory at the right hand of God, the Father. Christ is the eternal high priest, continually interceding before the Father for all men and women. "His power to save is utterly certain, since he is living for ever to intercede for all who come to God through him" (Heb 7:25). Our prayer for others in the Eucharist is uttered with this absolute confidence in the power of the prayer of Christ himself.

When he was on earth Jesus interceded for everyone. His ministry started with forty days of prayer and fasting in the desert. He interceded all night before choosing his apostles (Lk 6:12-13). At the Last Supper Jesus predicted that Peter and others would be tested by Satan; but Jesus assured Peter, "I have prayed for you, Simon, that your faith may not fail" (Lk 22:31-32). In the priestly prayer at the

Supper, he prayed at length for his disciples, and especially for unity (Jn 17:6-26). He prayed fervently in the Garden of Gethsemane, and asked his disciples to pray with him (Mk 14:32-42). And on the cross he prayed forgiveness for his executioners. (Lk 23:34)

The passion of Christ, culminating in his death on the cross, was the greatest act of intercession by Jesus. By this our redemption was won. All that was needed for the salvation of humanity has been done. Praise be to Jesus! But there remains the great work of bringing all men and women to accept this gift of saving love won for us by Jesus. The ministry of intercession is paramount in this. We need to plug into the power of Jesus' priestly intercession which continues now and forever at the right hand of God. Paul says, "It is Christ Jesus who died, yes, who was raised, who is at the right hand of God, who indeed intercedes for us" (Rom 8:34). When we offer our prayers for others in the Mass we are joining with Jesus, in the "inner circle" as it were, sharing the same burden of Jesus for the salvation of others. Jesus "desires everyone to be saved and to come to the knowledge of the truth" (1 Tim 2:4). In the Eucharist we cry out to God on behalf of those who are yet to open their hearts to the gospel message, and we can be utterly confident that our prayer is efficacious because it is the very prayer of Jesus himself. His power to save is utterly certain.

The Whole Church Prays

Hebrews says, "Let us therefore approach the throne of grace with boldness, so that we may receive mercy and find grace and help in time of need" (Heb 4:16). It is good to remember that, as we approach the throne of God all the saints, with the Blessed Mother, are with us, already adoring the Lamb that was slain and has now victory gained. Christ is the Head of the body, but the body has many parts. The celebrants of the Mass, who join with Christ, the High Priest, are not only those we can see around us, but also the invisible presence of all the communion of saints, including the martyrs, the Blessed Virgin Mary, and "a great multitude which no one could number, from every nation, from all tribes, and peoples and tongues". (Rev 7:9)[99]

In James it says, "The prayer of the righteous one is powerful in its effect" (James 5:16). The number of righteous ones in heaven is countless. What awesome prayer power! Add to this the reality that every Mass is not just offered by those assembled with us, but by the whole pilgrim Church, in communion with all the bishops, the successors of the apostles, and the Pope as the successor of Peter. When we get a vision of the prayer power involved we would be crazy not to capitalise on it by crying out with all our heart and mind and strength for those, whether alive or dead, who need to experience the mercy of God, confidently commending them into his loving hands.

God has chosen to act in this world through the mediation of human beings. He looks for an intercessor. Intercession is "standing between" the ones for whom we are praying and God, and seeking to have the fire of God's love come upon them in a real and concrete way. At the same time it is "standing between" these ones and Satan who comes to "steal, kill and destroy". We seek to protect them by the precious blood of Jesus, so they gain strength in the spiritual battle (Jn 10:10). Enlisting all the angels and saints and the Blessed Virgin Mary, as well as the whole pilgrim Church in its most powerful prayer, the Eucharist, is the surest way of victory. Yet it requires our sincere disposition of heart, joined to the heart of Jesus, the good Shepherd, who was wrenched in the stomach as he looked upon the crowds, because they were "harassed and dejected, like sheep without a shepherd". (Mt 9:36)

Confidence and Perseverance

It also requires perseverance. Jesus told the parable of the importunate neighbour who knocked on the door persistently even though it was seriously inconveniencing the occupants of the house. It was perseverance that led to the door being opened (Lk 11:5-8). He also told the parable of the widow pestering an unjust judge until he gave in to her just demands. "Now will not God see justice done to his chosen who cry to him day and night even when he delays to help them?" (Lk 18:1-8) It will be persistence that will win the day.

Because we are confident that the prayer of Jesus at the right hand of the Father is utterly certain to bring salvation, our intercession is a prayer of victory. Like Moses in the battle against the Amalekites we are to pray with hands outstretched believing in the victory of the Lord. When Moses, overlooking the battle on a nearby mountain, kept his arms raised in prayer to God for the victory, the Israelites had the upper hand in the battle. But when Moses' arms grew tired and he let them fall, the battle went in favour of the Amalekites. He needed his brothers Aaron and Hur to support his arms, to keep his hands raised in prayer, and the victory was assured. In the Eucharist we are not alone; we are helping one another "to lift our hands reverently in prayer" and to persevere on behalf of those who need our prayers most. Catherine of Siena likened her intercessory prayer to standing at the foot of the cross of Jesus and collecting in a basin his blood, and then casting the blood upon the hardened hearts of those for whom she was praying. She knew that by the power of the blood of Jesus even the heart that is as hard as a diamond will be cracked open and become pliable in the hands of the Saviour.

A Powerhouse of Prayer

Because the Eucharist is the presence of the perfect prayer of Jesus to the Father, we can be certain that Eucharistic adoration is a powerful means of intercession also. Everything we can say about the Eucharistic action in the Mass is found also in this wonderful devotion of adoring Jesus in the Blessed Sacrament. These days around the world the Catholic people are rediscovering Eucharistic adoration as a powerhouse of prayer for the new evangelisation. Many places now have perpetual adoration. As he promised, when we lift up Jesus he draws all to himself. How true this is. Eucharistic adoration draws hearts to Jesus, and in and through this union with Jesus, prayer for others becomes mightily effective. So whether it is through the intercessory prayers in the Eucharistic liturgy, or through quiet contemplative prayer before the Blessed Sacrament, the cries of our hearts are one with the heart of Jesus as he continues to "thirst" for the souls of all men and women and to intercede for them before the Father.

19

BREAD FOR THE HUNGRY

"Give them something to eat." (Mk 6:37)

Five Loaves and Two Fish

The significance of the gospel accounts of the multiplication of the loaves and fish is not so much that it was a wonderful miracle. Let's look for the deeper meaning (Mk 6:35-44). The disciples were worried. It was a lonely hillside, the hour was late, and the people had nothing to eat. They came to Jesus, asking him to send the people away to go to the farms and villages around about to buy something to eat. Jesus' reply to his hapless disciples was, "Give them something to eat yourselves." The disciples were flabbergasted. That was impossible. There were "five thousand men", let alone women and children. Even if they found available food, how could they afford to buy so much? Notice that Jesus does not withdraw his original command. But he asks them how much food do they have? There were five loaves and two fish. Then Jesus had them sit down on the ground. He "*took* the five loaves and two fish, raised his eyes to heaven and *said the blessing*; then he *broke* the loaves and gave them".

While this event was not Eucharist, there is little doubt that in remembering the story the gospel writer is giving this account a Eucharistic meaning. We are meant to notice that Jesus did not hand the broken loaves to the crowd. Rather he handed them *to the disciples*. He was helping them fulfil his original command, "Give them something to eat." The miracle took place at the hands of the disciples as they distributed the loaves. It was a lesson in discipleship. They were always to be ready to give bread to the hungry. And because it has such strong Eucharistic overtones we can deduce that to celebrate Eucharist we become a community of disciples who are empowered to feed the poor. Jesus himself is bread for the hungry, the true sustenance for true human life in the world. The disciples learnt that they only had to come to Jesus and bring what little they had, and by his generous heart of love what they had would become more than enough, as long as they kept giving of themselves more and more.

In the first instance the accounts of Jesus feeding the multitudes speak of the Eucharist as food and nourishment for the journey of life. We are strengthened and given courage on our pilgrim journey. As recipients of the Bread of life we are sustained in our spiritual journey. We are consoled in our times of sorrow, emboldened in times of weakness, encouraged in times of disappointment and disillusionment. However, these biblical stories carry a further meaning. The full purpose of the Eucharist is not to leave us as passive recipients, gladly benefitting from the largesse of God's mercy and love. Yes, we must first receive, but so that we can give. "You received without charge, give without charge" (Mt 10:8). The power of love in the Eucharist is first a centripetal force drawing us closely into intimacy with Jesus and the fullness of the Father's love, but then it is a centrifugal force thrusting us out beyond ourselves to become bread of life for others.

If we willingly join with the sacrifice of Jesus on the cross, "passing over" with him to fullness of life with the Father, then it is impossible to leave behind the poor and oppressed of the world. To accept the bread of the Eucharist is to accept *to be bread* and sustenance for the poor of the world. Jesus crucified is above all representative of the marginalised, despised and oppressed of the world, of those who "don't count", who are easily neglected and disposed of. It was these who he was in solidarity with when he hung despised and rejected on the cross. He became one of them. In Eucharist we receive his mercy flowing from his pierced side on the cross because we too are broken and needy and deeply poor. But drawn into his heart we find ourselves radically turned outward towards others who are lost, alienated, and disorientated, crying out for their rights to be acknowledged and their dignity respected.

A Community which is Home for the Poor

A genuine Eucharistic community is one where the poor can feel accepted and find a home. This would be "the greatest and most effective presentation of the good news of the kingdom".[100] In the early Church love for the poor was the criterion for the authenticity of the gospel. When Peter and Paul met in Jerusalem they accepted they had different apostolates, but one thing they agreed was indispensable – "that they remember to help the poor" (Gal 2:10). This option was in the face of a pagan society with a highly self-centred way of life, and no room for the poor. This applies to our situation today. In the face of a society that can be geared towards wealth, power and prestige, we must be radically for the least, the weak, and the discarded. The Church's preferential option for the poor is founded in God's own identification with the poor. Jesus did not cling to his equality with the Father, but "emptied himself", becoming one with us. Paul reminds us that the Lord Jesus Christ was so generous "that though he was rich for your sakes he became poor, so that by his poverty you might become rich". (2 Cor 8:9)

In the celebration of Eucharist in early times the faithful brought up gifts of food for the poor with the bread and wine in the offertory procession. This was a clear sign that the community believed that when they received the body and blood of Christ, it was not only an interior and personal communion. It was also a moment of communion with the compassionate heart of the crucified Jesus for those who were the least fortunate in their midst. When the procession took place it was understood to be an action of the whole community, offering itself on the altar in union with the offering of Jesus. St. Justin tells us that when the gifts came forward it always included gifts for the sustenance of the weakest in the community:

> Those who are well off, and who are also willing, give as each chooses. What is gathered is given to him who presides to assist orphans and widows, those whom illness or any other cause has deprived of resources, prisoners, immigrants, and, in a word, all who are in need.[101]

In this joyful ritual offering, the community was connecting its heart with that of Jesus. As Jesus died on the cross for love of his own, so they would die to themselves through generous giving and love for one another, and especially for the weakest of their members.

Priority to the Poor

Jesus' command to his disciples, "You yourselves give them something to eat!" goes even further than care for the least in our Christian communities. It means that our genuinely Eucharistic communities will not be insulated from the poor beyond our membership. They will not be like the rich man who was oblivious and indifferent to the Lazarus at his door. Our communities that celebrate Eucharist will be growing more deeply in the merciful heart of Jesus and be attuned to the cry of the poor, wherever they may be. Rather than living as if behind windows with "double glazing", shut out from the desperate cry of the homeless and afflicted, they will be in genuine solidarity with the poor. This means "working to eliminate the structural causes of poverty and to promote the integral development of the poor".[102] It means giving priority to the needs of the poor, and a generous redistribution of goods in favour of the poor. But even before this necessary action for justice, it means a sincere change of heart in us so that we come to realise that the poor are *our people*. It is not a matter of "us" who have much, who will care for "them" who have little. Rather it is a deep realisation on the part of the Eucharistic community that we are one, and all-inclusive. There is a mutual reciprocity in relationship. If we reach out to those who are needy we find that we are ministered to ourselves. We are all together in Christ in a mysterious way.

Pope Francis speaks of a "loving attentiveness" to the poor, not in any way tinged with condescension, but a love which genuinely esteems the other as a person of highest value. So it is not primarily in activities and programs that the change will happen, but in the overflow of love from the heart of Jesus, still carrying the wounds of his sacrifice, whom we encounter in Eucharist. Suffused with his self-giving love we cherish all those for whom he died, that is everyone we meet. The homeless, the addicted, refugees, the isolated and abandoned, all are our people. Pope Francis says, "Sometimes we are tempted to be that kind of Christian who keeps the Lord's wounds at arm's length. Yet Jesus wants us to touch human misery, to touch the suffering flesh of others."[103] And he assures us that when we come into personal contact with the suffering of others we "touch the suffering flesh of Christ".

"You did it to Me"

Through his becoming one flesh with us and through his death and resurrection Jesus has identified himself with the poor. Matthew's last judgement text spells this out, "As often as you did it to the least of my brethren you did it to me" (Mt 25:35-45). In the poor we have a real presence of Christ; not in the same way as in the unique Eucharistic presence, but still real indeed. Jesus instituted this sign of himself as he instituted the Eucharist. He who pronounced the words over the bread, "This is my body" said these same words referring to the poor. As Mother Teresa used to say, we meet him in "the distressing disguise of the poor". This is where we touch the "suffering flesh of Christ". What is done to a poor person is done to Christ. Mother Teresa used to encourage her sisters to do the "five finger" test at the end of each day. Firstly look back over the day and all the various encounters you have made with a whole range of people. Then apply the test to each of these encounters. Five key words for each encounter; one word for each finger, "You-did-it-to-me."

Mother Teresa once told a story of a young sister who was having difficulty being able to recognise the presence of Jesus in the derelict and dying men who they were picking up from the streets of Calcutta to take to the hospice for the dying. The novice was naturally repulsed by the smell and disfigurement of these most abandoned ones. Mother instructed the sister to look closely at the priest during the Eucharist the next morning; see how reverently he handles the sacred host, which is the real presence of Jesus. Then do the same when she meets the broken men on the streets. The sister did as she was told and she came home that day after cleansing the ugly wounds of a man who was dying. She was so happy, because as she held this man and ministered to him with the same reverence and care with which the priest held Jesus in the Eucharist, she had a moment of gracious revelation; she realised she was actually holding Jesus. And her heart filled with love and compassion for this wretched man. Her vocation was born again.

When we celebrate Eucharist we are participating in the loving embrace of Jesus for all men and women, and especially for the poor. In a very real way they are part of the Church, and so they are our brothers and sisters in Christ. Christ has declared them as his body; to touch them is to touch him. Whether they believe in Christ or not, they belong in a special way to him, and hence to his Church. We are the Church *for* the poor and *of* the poor. But this does not only mean the poor of the Church, but also the poor of the world, whether they are baptised or not. They belong to the Church not because they have declared they belong to Christ, but because Christ has declared they belong to him: "You did it to me". This injunction does not only refer to the baptised, but to all persons.

Champions of the Poor

St Laurence, the deacon, in the year 258 was weeping as Pope Sixtus IV was being led to martyrdom, crying out, "Father, where are you going without your deacon?" The Pope answered, "I am not leaving you, my son. You shall follow me in three days." Laurence then informed the Roman prefect that he wanted to show him the secret treasures of the Church. If he came to meet Laurence at a certain time he would be able to receive the Church's greatest treasures. Meanwhile Laurence, who was in charge of the practical support of the poor, gathered together all of those who were receiving alms from the Church. When the Prefect arrived at the appointed time he found a large band of men and women in tattered clothing with uncouth manners and raucous laughter. The Prefect was put out by this miserable spectacle of broken humanity. He rebuked Lawrence, "You said you would hand over to me the treasures of the Church. Where are they?" Lawrence replied, "Here they are, your Excellency! These are the treasures of the Church!" Needless to say Lawrence had the honour of following his bishop to execution as a martyr. Tradition tells us he was slowly burnt to death on a large gridiron with glowing coals under it. As his body was cooking he is reputed to have said with jest, "You can turn me over now; this side has been cooked well enough!" The Church's greatest treasures are the very least and the most needy.

St John Chrysostom, the preacher with the "golden voice" did not mince his words with his congregation. He was never more eloquent than when calling them to account for a false religion which adorned the Church's architecture and liturgy, but ignored the poor. Speaking in the context of the Mass he thundered:

> This mystery does not permit us to chase after wealth by unjust means ... Let us flee then from this abyss; neither let us think it sufficient for our salvation, if after we have robbed widows and orphans, we offer for the altar a gold and bejeweled chalice ... For the church is not a gold or silver boutique ... That table at the Last Supper was not of silver nor was the cup of gold, out of which Christ gave his disciples his own blood; but it was nonetheless precious and awesome because it was full of the Holy Spirit. Do you wish to honour Christ's body? Don't pass by him when you see him naked; do not honour him here in the church with silken garments, while you neglect him perishing outside from the cold and nakedness! For he that said, "This is my body," and by his work confirmed the fact, this same one said, "You saw me starving, and fed me not;" and, "In as much as you did not do it to one of the least of these, you did not do it to me." For this purpose there is no need of silk coverings, but indeed a pure soul ... God has no need of golden chalices, but of golden souls.[104]

The Banquet of Life

The whole of our life can be imaged as a meal set before us as a gift from our loving Father, God. God's vision for the world is that human beings all share in this banquet. Unfortunately selfishness and greed have made it a planet of "haves" and "have nots". Less than half of the huge sums of money spent worldwide on armaments would be more than enough to rescue the world's poor from destitution and end the scandal of hunger and malnutrition afflicting millions in the world today. This situation is totally contrary to the loving plan of God. As John Paul II said, all human beings are to be made "sharers on a par with ourselves, in the banquet of life to which all are equally invited by God".[105] By ourselves we are helpless to right the wrong of human selfishness. But Christ's sacrifice on the cross, purchased for us with the price of his blood, gives us a new way of being together. His selfless offering was the birthing of a new world. The dream of the banquet, for which Jesus died, can have reality now to the extent that we join him and die to ourselves and live for one another. His sacrifice has given us the power to do just that. We will no longer be indifferent to the problems of the world where so many are excluded from sharing in the banquet of life. Eucharist invites us into communion with Christ given for us, and becoming one with him means we share in his sacrifice, giving ourselves as bread for a hungry world.

20

RECONCILIATION AND PEACE

"Blessed are the peacemakers, for they shall be called children of God." (Mt 5:9)

Peace on Earth

When the shepherds in the fields had heard from an angel that the Saviour had been born in the nearby town of Bethlehem, the city of David, we are told a huge choir of angels began singing, "Glory to God in the highest heavens and peace on earth to all who enjoy his favour" (Lk 2:14). They proclaimed the promise of peace brought into the world by Jesus, the incarnate Son of God, as sheer gift to all who are open to receive it. In these days billions of people on earth are longing desperately for peace. At the time of writing the self-proclaimed Islamic State is slaughtering minorities, including Christians and adherents of other Islamic sects. In Nigeria the Boko Haram are terrorising Christians, abducting young women as sex slaves and burning churches. In Pakistan and Afghanistan the Taliban are claiming responsibility for carnage in schools, and in many locations there is an ever increasing number of suicide bombers. Palestinians and Israelis remain in a tense stand-off, with mutual hatred having been bred into a whole generation of people. Is peace possible in our troubled world?

The Messianic prophecies in the Old Testament looked forward to a new era of peace. "They shall beat their swords into ploughshares, and their spears into pruning hooks; nation shall not lift up sword against nation, neither shall they learn war anymore" (Is 2:4). Is this just pious wishful thinking? No. We believe that the prophecy refers to Jesus as the way of peace. "For there is a child born to us, a son given to us, and dominion is laid on his shoulders; and this is the name they give him: wonder-counsellor, Mighty God, Eternal Father, Prince of Peace. Wide is his dominion in a peace that has no end" (Is 9:5-6). The Eucharist opens up this way of peace.

The original problem for humanity arose at the very beginning. In Genesis we read that Adam and Eve, representing the whole of the human race, did not trust God, but rebelled against God, and disobeyed his command. The consequence of loss of God was dislocation in our relationships with one another, with ourselves and with creation (Gen 3:1-24). To save his skin Adam blamed Eve for the problem, "It was that woman you put me with." Now there was also disharmony with creation: "You shall work by the sweat of your brow ... and your work on the earth will yield brambles and thistles." And there was interior dislocation as well; they felt their nakedness; shame and guilt entered into the human race. Enmity and jealousy arose in the human heart; Cain murdered his brother Abel because he seemed more favoured by God. The story of the human race as a result of the fall is one of hearts prone to anger, bitterness, revenge, hatred, and envy, all too often leading to unspeakable atrocities and crimes in personal relationships, in communal and societal and international affairs. How can this come to an end? Where is the possibility of redemption? Thanks be to God for Jesus Christ, our redeemer. Each time we celebrate Eucharist we touch into this redeeming work of Christ and seek to apply its fruits to our broken world.

Peace by His Blood

I began this chapter by focusing on the child Jesus in Bethlehem as a sign of peace. He is the "prince of peace", but with a difference. He did not come with an army to force his rule on others; nor was he born in a palace. Rather he was born in a stable and laid in a feeding trough for animals; a Saviour who would turn around our hopeless situation not by force but by the persuasion of humility and love. But it was not enough for him to take on human flesh as a child. He was born to die. The peace that he came to win for us would only be accomplished by his death on Calvary. The rule of violence had to be decisively broken.

As a result of mankind's sin the cycle of violence has been perpetuated down through the centuries. We see it at the macro level amongst nations, but also in our own relationships in family and community. So often there is a break-down in relationship through conflict that remains unresolved. The only way through is by mutual forgiveness, restoration of trust, and learning to walk together again. But it all seems so hard and next to impossible to achieve. How can peace come? We proclaim that Jesus won peace for us by his blood on the cross (Col 1:20). How did this happen? He allowed all the hatred, jealousy, anger, contempt, torture and rejection of his human dignity to assail him. He chose not to use the power that was within his grasp to retaliate and take revenge on the perpetrators of the violence.

Here we could maybe draw upon a theory of violence presented by Rene Girard, a French thinker.[106] He argues that throughout the history of humanity violence has originated from different people, or groups of people, desiring and actively seeking to acquire the same object and coming into conflict as a result. He then suggests that world religions themselves have historically promoted a violent way of resolving the tensions involved in these conflicts by sacrificing animals or even human beings as a "scapegoat". So rather than heal the problem of violence, religion has added to the ongoing cycle.

However, Girard, having been himself converted to Christianity, proclaims that the sacrifice of Jesus on the cross is radically different from any sacrifice that preceded it, even those in the Old Testament Temple tradition. What is different? The sacrifice of Jesus is the voluntary offering of himself on our behalf. It is his self-offering of love, willing to be immolated for our sake, by taking all the violence upon himself. He absorbed all the violence into himself and hence put it to death with him. Now, through the death of Jesus, *the cycle of violence has been broken*. Rather than meet hatred with hatred, he met it with love. Rather than meet violence with revenge, he met it with forgiveness. "Father, forgive them for they know not what they are doing." He made himself the voluntary "scapegoat" of humanity, the innocent victim of all violence.

God was Reconciling us

Jesus did not prepare animals to be victims to offer to the Father. His offering on the cross was not a sacrifice like the ancient religions when they offered something up and destroyed it as an attempt to appease an angry God. In fact, the offering of Jesus on the Cross was not because we needed to do something to placate God, but rather it was God himself acting to save us from our wretchedness. The Eucharist is the primary sacrament of reconciliation, since it re-presents in a ritual and unbloody manner the once for all sacrifice of Jesus on the cross. His sacrifice has brought us peace. As Paul says:

> It is all God's work. It was God who reconciled us to himself through Christ and gave us the work of handing on this reconciliation. In other words, God in Christ was reconciling the world to himself, not holding men's faults against them, and he has entrusted to us the news that they are reconciled ... and the appeal we make in Christ's name is: be reconciled to God. (2 Cor 5:18-19)

In every Eucharist this is what is proclaimed. We find the power to be reconciled in a deeper way to God, and hence find the power to be restored in our relationships with one another. To recognise this dynamic the Church has composed two beautiful Eucharistic Prayers of Reconciliation.

A Change of Heart

Peace only comes through forgiveness and reconciliation. In 1996 as a result of the Port Arthur massacre the Australian government put in place strong gun laws and designated an amnesty time for those who possessed fire-arms to hand them in to authorities. So many people came forward with their lethal weapons and submitted them, receiving an appropriate compensation for their loss. This could be an image of what needs to happen at each Eucharist. We need to bring our lethal weapons and lay them at the feet of Jesus, the Prince of peace. I am not meaning actual firearms, but rather the "weapons" in the heart that we are carrying around ready to do damage to others. We may never assassinate anyone with a high powered rifle, but we may willingly assassinate their good name out of cold anger and revenge. We may never fire a pistol at point blank range at anyone, but we may well speak words of hot anger and rage which cause destruction. Or maybe we simply harbour deep grudges, bitterness and unforgiveness in the heart. The issue of violence in the world is about what we carry in our hearts. This is why we begin the celebration of Eucharist with a liturgy of repentance. Jesus said, "If you are bringing your offering to the altar and your brother has something against you, leave your offering there before the altar, go and be reconciled with your brother first, and then come back and present your offering" (Mt 5:23-24). In other words, to be able to enter into the sacrament with sincerity and right intention, we must have a heart desiring reconciliation, and willing to do something about it. Then the offering of ourselves will be genuine and the Eucharist will be a powerful means of empowering us to deepen in this spirit of reconciliation.

Build Bridges not Walls

We recently celebrated 25 years since the dismantling of the Berlin Wall which had become a symbol of ideological division and hatred. Yet, humanity continues to build walls, such as the wall that now divides

Bethlehem, the town of the birth of the Saviour, and Jerusalem, where he died and rose for us. When Pope Francis was passing through the check point which regulates who passes through the wall to go from Bethlehem to Jerusalem, he called for an unscheduled stop. Leaning his head against the wall, this symbol of enmity and division, he quietly prayed. Peace will not come through building walls, but by building bridges.

For Paul the peace that Jesus won on the cross was applied immediately to the division in the early Church between Jews and Gentiles. There is a beautiful text in the Letter to the Ephesians:

> For he (Christ) is our peace, who has made us both one, and has broken down the dividing wall of hostility, by abolishing in his flesh 'the law of commandments and ordinances', that he might create in himself one new man in place of the two, so making peace, and might reconcile us both to God in one body, through the cross, thereby bringing hostility to an end. (Eph 2:14-16)

Paul is referring to the hostility between Jew and Gentile, between circumcised and uncircumcised. Some commentators believe that Paul was thinking of the wall in the Temple in Jerusalem which separated the court of the Gentiles from the inner court of the Jews. There was a sign over the door to the inner sanctuary warning that any uncircumcised man who passed through that door would be put to death. This is a reminder to us that religion itself can through prejudice and sectarianism build walls against others. These walls must be demolished by the power of love and reconciliation. In our own lives also we can be building walls to protect ourselves from others, or to perpetuate our enmity towards them. To celebrate Eucharist means to allow the walls of hatred, prejudice and division to be broken down by the presence of Christ and the power of his death and resurrection.

Peace be with you

In the evening of the day of the resurrection Jesus appeared to the apostles huddled behind closed doors "for fear of the Jews" (Jn 20:19-20). He said, "Peace be with you" and showed them his wounds. This word of peace, "*shalom*", was even more powerful because of where he had been. He had gone to the worst of human darkness and despair, but had retained his trust in the Father. He had been hanging on the cross carrying the weight of all the human atrocities that in our broken condition we have committed against one another. And from that place he had risen; he had conquered hatred by love. And now he breathed the Spirit upon them, bringing them the peace that was won by the cross. And he gave them the ministry of bringing this peace through the forgiveness of sins. In Eucharist we find this peace. We receive the prince of peace into our hearts. At the Last Supper, before returning to the Father, Jesus promised, "Peace I leave you, my own peace I give to you. Not as the world gives do I give it to you. Do not let your hearts be troubled or afraid" (Jn 14:27). This *shalom* in the biblical language carries with it the promise of reconciliation between humanity and God, and consequently a new harmony within our own hearts, and a new harmony in our relationships with one another, and indeed a new harmony with the whole of creation. Christ was "the first to be born from the dead" and it was God's purpose that "all things be reconciled through him and for him, everything in heaven and everything on earth, when he made peace by the blood of his cross". (Col 1:20)

Changing the World

Throughout the book I have been intent upon opening our hearts more to the wonder of the Eucharist. It is fitting to end on a proclamation of the cosmic dimensions of this mystery. Eucharist is at the centre of the Church's life, worship and mission. Indeed it is at the centre of the universe, already the beginning of the "new heaven and new earth". As Pope John Paul II reminded us "even when it is celebrated on a humble altar of a country church, the Eucharist is always in some way celebrated *on the altar of the world!* It unites heaven and earth. It embraces and permeates all creation".[107]

On Mount Tabor the apostles saw Christ transfigured. For one blinding moment something of the inner reality of Christ, hidden from them through the ordinariness of life, suddenly shone splendidly before them. The veil was lifted for a brief instant and they saw the glory of his divinity shining through his flesh. It was as dazzling as the sun. In heaven we will experience something akin to this as we gaze upon the glory shining on the face of Christ. "Then shall the just shine as the sun in the kingdom of the Father" (Mt 13:43). The Blessed Virgin Mary has already experienced this; and we also are destined for glory.

When the Word was made flesh in the womb of Mary it was not just a wonder for a day, and then it was over. It was the beginning of a transformation of all humanity. All flesh, all humankind, is to be lifted up into the divine presence. "Eye has not seen, nor ear heard, nor heart of man conceived, what God has in store for those who love him" (1 Cor 2:9). We will all be transfigured: "Heaven is where we belong, and from there we are expecting a Saviour, the Lord Jesus Christ, who will transfigure these bodies of our lowliness to be like his glorious body, according to the power by which he can subdue all things to himself" (Phil 3:20). Tabor not only reveals Christ in glory, but gives us a glimpse of what we ourselves will become.

This transfiguration is destined to go beyond us to the whole of creation. Everything will be brought together and restored in Christ, the beginning and the end of all things (Eph 1:10). This process of transformation is already underway. By making his love a reality among us Christ is changing the world. We are being transfigured through the new life he gives us, and especially through the gift of himself in

Eucharist. We grow in his love and we are changed. The Eucharist is at the centre of this transfiguration of the world. This sacrament is a preparation for "the new heaven and the new earth". One day Christ will transfigure our wretched bodies into copies of his own glorious body, and with the same power he will also transfigure the entire universe. This transfiguration of the universe began with the bodily resurrection of Jesus. It is continued in every Mass as the bread and wine are changed into his body and blood. As his divinity shone through his body on Mt Tabor, so it is present in every consecrated host, and has changed it into his flesh and blood. With awe and wonder we celebrate the Eucharist at the heart of the universe, with the sure hope of a new humanity won for us in the bodily resurrected Christ, and with the pledge of a future glory beyond our imagining, when the whole of created reality will be transformed into glory.

ENDNOTES

1 Vatican II, *Presbyterorum Ordinis*, 5
2 *Catechism of the Catholic Church*, 1327
3 Pope John Paul II, *Mane Nobiscum Domine*, 1
4 Pope Benedict XVI, *Sacramentum Caritatis*, 56
5 Vatican Council II, *Dei Verbum*, 21
6 Ibid
7 Pope Benedict VI, *Verbum Dei*, 54
8 Ibid, 55
9 Ibid, 86
10 Ibid, 59
11 Pope Francis, *Evangelii Gaudium*, 138
12 Ibid, 137.
13 Ibid, 146
14 Ibid, 151
15 Vatican Council II, *Lumen Gentium*, 11
16 Paul Hinnebusch OP, *Praise: a Way of Life* (Ann Arbor, Michigan: Word of Life, 1976): 3
17 Pope Francis, Praise is not just for Charismatics, Zenit.org (Vatican City, 28 January 2014)
18 Hinnebusch, op cit, p. 41
19 Ibid, p. 43
20 Ibid, pp. 47-8
21 Vatican II, *Sacrosanctum Concilium*, 7
22 *Catechism of the Catholic Church*, 1082
23 Pope Benedict XVI, *Deus Caritas Est*, 12

24 Pope John Paul II, Homily, Shrine of Divine Mercy, Krakow, 22 April 2001

25 *Catechism of the Catholic Church*, 1367

26 The precise moment that we understand this occurs is when the words of the priest are spoken in the name of Christ at the consecration. Without this we do not have validity. However, in contemporary perspective it adds richness to our sacrificial engagement if we don't focus just on the essentials, but have a more all-embracing appreciation of the overall movement of the liturgy as we worship the Father in and through Jesus by the power of the Holy Spirit.

27 Raniero Cantalamessa, *The Eucharist Our Sanctification* (Manila: St Paul's, 2006), p. 9

28 *Catechism of the Catholic Church*, 1368

29 Pope Benedict XVI, *Deus Caritas Est*, 13

30 Pope Benedict XVI, Homily Marienfeld, WYD, Cologne, 21 August 2005

31 Ibid

32 See Fr Ken Barker, *Becoming Fire* (Melbourne: Freedom Publishing, 2001)

33 Ibid, 14

34 Pastor Richard Wurmbrand, "An Undying Love", *Again* magazine, September 1987

35 Martyrdom of Polycarp, 13 *Early Christian Writings* (NY: Penguin, 1968) p. 160

36 Ignatius of Antioch, *Letter to the Romans*, 4

37 Given in Sheila Cassidy, *Good Friday People* (London: Darton, Longman and Todd, 1991) p. 130

38 St Thérèse of Lisieux, *Story of a Soul* (Washington DC: ICS Publications, 1976) p. 77

39 Cyril of Alexandria, Commentary on John IV, 2.

40 St Ephrem the Syrian, *Sermons for Holy Week*, 4, 4

41 Thomas Aquinas, *Summa Theologica*, q.79, a.1, ad2

42 St Ambrose, *On the Sacraments*, V, 17

43 *Paschal Homilies in the tradition of Origen*, II, 7

44 St Ephrem the Syrian, *Sermon for the Holy Week*, 2, 627

45 St Thérèse of Lisieux, *Story of a Soul*, p. 98

46 St Gregory the Great, *On the Passion*, Sermon 12, 7

47 St Augustine, *Confessions*, 7, 10

48 Pope John Paul II, *Dies Domini*, 46

49 Francis Xavier Nguyen Van Thuan, *Testimony of Hope* (Boston: Pauline books, 2000) p. 131

50 St Catherine of Siena, *The Dialogue*, 55

51 Ibid, 129

52 St Catherine of Siena, *Letter*, 120

53 *Catechism of the Catholic Church*, 1393

54 St Ambrose, *On the Sacraments*, IV, 6, 28

55 SCR, *Eucharisticum Mysterium*, 1967, 32

56 *Catechism of the Catholic Church*, 1140

57 St Augustine, *Sermon*, 272

58 St Augustine, *Sermon Denis*, 6

59 Pope Francis, *Evangelii Gaudium*, 47

60 Jean Vanier, *The Eucharist: Gift from God Par Excellence*, 49th Eucharistic Congress, Quebec, June 2008.

61 Francis of Assisi, *Letter to General Chapter*, 2, Writings, 106

62 Pope Paul VI, *Mysterium Fidei*, 39

63 Justin Martyr, *Apologia* 1, 66-7

64 Cyril of Jerusalem, *Catechetical Discourses*, 22, *Mystagogia*, 4, 3-6

65 St Ambrose, *On the Sacraments*, IV, 14-16

66 St John Chrysostom, *De Proditione Judae*, 1, 6

67 St Augustine, *Sermon*, 229

68 Theodore of Mopsuestia, *Catecheses*, XVI, 11ff.

69 *Catechism of the Catholic Church*, 1375

70 *Enchiridion Symbolorum*, ed. Denzinger and Schonmetzer, (DS), 690

71 Ibid

72 Attributed to Thomas Aquinas. This translation by Gerard Manley Hopkins

73 Council of Trent, DS 1642

74 Council of Trent, DS 1651

75 This quote and the following are from Andre Frossard, *God Exists: I Have Met Him*, e-book: godexists.yolasite.com

76 Alphonsus Liguori, *Visit to the Blessed Sacrament*

77 Pope John Paul II, *Ecclesia de Eucharistia*, 25

78 Sacred Congregation for Divine Worship, *Eucharistiae Sacramentum*, 1973, 80

79 Ibid

80 St Bonaventure, *The Mind's Journey toward God*, III, 5

81 St Bernard of Clairvaux, *Commentary on the Song of Songs*, 61, 4

82 Vincent Kerns, *St Margaret Mary* (London: Darton, Longman and Todd, 1961) pp. 44-5

83 Jean-Jacques Antier, *Charles de Foucauld* (San Francisco: Ignatius Press, 1997) p. 154

84 Ibid, p. 223

85 Pope Benedict XVI, *Sacramentum Caritatis*, 84

86 Pope Paul VI, *Evangelii Nuntiandi*, 14

87 Pope Francis, *Evangelii Gaudium*, 24

88 Pope Benedict XVI, *Sacramentum Caritatis*, 86

89 Pope Francis, *Evangelii Gaudium*, 49

90 Pope Paul VI, *Evangelii Nuntiandi*, 24

91 An example of an experiment in this direction can be found in Michael White and Tom Corcoran, *Rebuilt* (Indiana: Ave Maria Press, 2013)

92 Sister Briege McKenna, *Miracles Do Happen* (Dublin: Veritas Publications, 1978) pp. 67-8

93 Emilien Tardif, *Jesus is the Messiah* (Melbourne: Manna Publications, 1991) pp. 41-2

94 See Paul Glynn, *The Wayside Stream* (Hunters Hill, Marist Fathers, 2003) pp. 98-107

95 Ignatius of Antioch, *Letter to the Ephesians*, 20

96 Embolism in the *Roman Missal*

97 Pope Benedict XVI, *Sacramentum Caritatis*, 8

98 Pope John Paul II, Wednesday Audience, 1983

99 *Catechism of the Catholic Church*, 1138

100 Pope John Paul II, *Novo Millennio Ineunte*, 50

101 Justin Martyr, *Apologia*, 1, 67

102 Pope Francis, *Evangelii Gaudium*, 188

103 Ibid, 270

104 St John Chrysostom, *Homilies on the Gospel of Matthew*, 50, 3-4

105 Pope John Paul II, *Sollicitudo Rei Socialis*, 39

106 Rene Girard, *The Scapegoat* (Baltimore: Johns Hopkins University Press, 1977); Willard Swartley ed., *Violence Renounced: Rene Girard, Biblical Studies and Peacemaking* (Telford: Pandora Press, 2000)

107 Pope John Paul II, *Ecclesia de Eucharistia*, 8